BOOKS BY

Abbot Vonier

A Key to the Doctrine of the Eucharist

The Human Soul

The Personality of Christ

The Christian Mind

The Divine Motherhood

The Life of the World to Come

The Art of Christ: Retreat Conferences

The Angels

The New and Eternal Covenant

Christ, the King of Glory

The Victory of Christ

The Spirit and the Bride

The People of God

Sketches and Studies in Theology

CHRISTIANUS
The Christian Life

ABBOT VONIER

ZACCHEUS PRESS

Bethesda

Nihil Obstat: Georgius D. Smith, S.T.D., Ph.D.
                   Deputy Censor
Imprimatur: Joseph Butt
                   Vicar General
                   Westminster, June 19, 1933

ZACCHEUS PRESS and the colophon are trademarks of Zaccheus Press. The Zaccheus Press colophon was designed by Michelle Dick.

Scripture quotations are from the Douay-Rheims translation of the Bible. The text is set in Garamond.

Library of Congress Cataloging-in-Publication Data

Vonier, Anscar, 1875-1938.
    Christianus : the Christian life / Abbot Vonier.
        p. cm.
    ISBN 978-0-9830297-2-4 (alk. paper)
    1. Christian life--Catholic authors. I. Title.
    BX2350.3.V67 2011
    248.4'82--dc23
                                                    2011033354

10 9 8 7 6 5 4 3 2 1

To learn more about Abbot Vonier, please visit our webpage:

www.zaccheuspress.com

PATER MISERICORDIAE, EMITTE SPIRITUM TUUM UT OMNIUM HUNC
LIBRUM LEGENTIUM ET ANIMUM ILLUMINET ET COR TANGAT.
SIT RATIO ET VIA AD EXAEDIFICANDUM REGNUM TUUM.
PER CHRISTUM DOMINUM NOSTRUM. AMEN.

Contents

Introduction

It is difficult for a Christian writer to encounter the works of Abbot Vonier without mixed feelings. For those of us who grew up in the wake of Vatican II, when so many great Catholic authors were forgotten, the lacuna of our religious education led us to believe that we could write great books, perhaps even timeless books, about God and the life of the Christian soul. After all, many of us were raised, even in Catholic schools, without knowledge of G.K. Chesterton, Dietrich Von Hildebrand, Jacques Maritain or other lights of the Catholic intellectual renaissance of the early 20th century. We were led to think that we could make our mark. Sure, there was C.S. Lewis—we read *The Screwtape Letters* in my Catholic high school—but who else?

Then, about 20 years ago, I began to discover a lost world. While going through my father's things after his death in 1996, I came across a copy of Chesterton's *Orthodoxy*. In 2001 a new edition of Dietrich Von Hildebrand's *Transformation in Christ* was issued. More books followed. For the first time I heard names like Frank Sheed, Columba Marmion, Hilaire Belloc and Christopher Dawson. As a Catholic journalist who hoped to write books about the Church myself, the effect of this avalanche of genius was both delight and despair. It was like hoping to play professional football and discovering that the NFL exists.

Now, with the publication of *Christianus: The Christian Life*, the task gets harder still. This is muscular, penetrating, timeless writing. And like most great writing, it has the ability to tell you something you already know yet make it seem as though you are hearing it for the first time. For example, as Christians we all know we are called to be disciples of Christ. But what does that mean? To Abbot Vonier, it means that everything else is secondary:

> When the Son of God says that in this is the Father glorified, that we should become His disciples, He has indeed opened out for us infinite vistas and glorious possibilities.... Christian discipleship means being called to witness the miracle at the marriage feast of Cana and climbing Mount Tabor; being made to share the great Pasch of the Passion and watching in the Garden of Gethsemane; being met by the Risen Christ and being led by Him to the hilltop of the Ascension; being ordered to the Upper Room where the Spirit is to manifest Himself and being a partaker in a thousand other things, one more marvelous than the other. Who cannot see at a glance that Christian discipleship has no equal on earth nor rival in history?

This passage, like so many in *Christianus*, gives the bracing intoxication of deep insight into a truth that we are already supposed to know.

Dom Anscar Vonier was fortunate to live and write at a time when most Catholics knew the faith and lived it with joy and intensity. Born in 1875, he was ordained priest in 1898, and elected Abbot of Buckfast Abbey, England, at the age of 31.

During his lifetime, he was known as a great preacher, as the rebuilder of Buckfast (which fell into ruins after Henry VIII wrested control of it), and as a popular Catholic author. His friend Wilfrid Upson, the Abbot of Prinknash, explained Vonier's literary activity in this way: "The ideal at which he aimed in all is books was to enable even simple people to talk of the things of their Faith... He wanted to see Catholics throughout the land familiar with what he called 'a Christian Classicism'— able to speak of our Faith with ease and facility. In fact, he wanted to get back to the strong Faith of the Middle Ages, when men did not doubt, because they *knew* the true implication of the Dogmas of the Church."

Vonier's first book, *The Human Soul*, was published in 1913. Over a dozen more would follow. It was the beginning of a great era of Catholic letters in England. During the inter-War years, Ronald Knox, G.K. Chesterton and Christopher Dawson would publish most of their finest work. Vonier's books deserve to be considered in the same rank as those giants. His work exemplifies a Catholicism that, contrary to the "modernists" of our age (and theirs), does not reject reason or human dignity. To the contrary, it fosters the intellect of that the unique and wonderful creature, part flesh and part spirit, that is man. In his book *On the Unseriousness of Human Affairs*, the great Georgetown Jesuit James V. Schall notes that to some philosophers and historians, human beings only began to make progress after the Middle Ages, when a vision that put religion at the center of life was slowly replaced by a scientific outlook that purported to free man from the chains of Christianity. Yet as Christian thinkers have argued, it was precisely the Christian understanding of the dignity of the person as an individual created by God, and Christian faith in the rationality of God's creation, that made scientific progress possible.

Christianus is a guide to Christian life as lived on the ground, as it were. Begun as a series of magazine articles which his publisher urged him to expand into a full-length book, its themes are set forth in the chapter titles, and include the meaning of work, attaining spiritual fruitfulness, and the problem of temptation, as well as prayer, repentance, and joy. He has some interesting things to say on the subject of citizenship that are still relevant, perhaps especially relevant, to Catholics living in modern-day America. In the final chapter he offers a calm, scriptural perspective on the much-vexed question of salvation outside the Church.

In treating all these subjects, Vonier's view is that the Christian life, the daily road to perfection, begins and ends in humble Christian discipleship.

That seems like an obvious point, but in our 21st Century post-Christian age even Catholics seem to have fumbled the basics. I recently read an article that, in an attempt to gain favor with a critic of the Catholic Church, advised the reader not to worry about orthodoxy too much—that "the Church has many faces." Such dilution, even—especially?—among Catholics is common today. An apparent road to enlightenment and tolerance, it actually shuts the door on the genuine joy that comes from a life lived in the truth. For in focusing on the many faces of the Church, we lose sight of the one face that matters: the face of Christ. As a great contemporary Catholic writer, George Weigel, reiterates in his recent *Letters to a Young Catholic*: looking at Christ, following Christ, is not an escape into fantasy, but a way of coming face to face with glorious reality.

Or as Abbot Vonier puts it in the third chapter of this book:

> The light of Christ is not only the guide to our steps, it is also a revealer of secrets. Through its power we see things as they

are. The light of Christ is therefore a thing of stern reality as well as of comfort. For this is the characteristic of true Christian illumination, that the mind of man has the courage to look at great truths and facts of divine justice and sanctity.

Reading *Christianus*, one is reintroduced to the reality of who we are. And for the believer of Vonier's time, as well as our own, "the certainties of the faith" produce "peace of soul."

The Church has a strange way at every discernible moment, not only of being complete, but of knowing herself to be complete; one might almost say she is perfectly satisfied with herself and thinks herself the mistress of souls, nay, even the queen of the world... Never does the Church look forward to some future liberation, as if in the actual present she were a slave to an alien and oppressive power. Human empires have known such periods, but not the empire of the Spirit. Nor does the Church ever pray for a band of heroes to come along and lead her to freedom and victory. She seems to be conscious that heroes are with her all the time, doing splendid service in her cause.

We cannot all be heroes. But in an age which sorely needs them, you will not find a better or surer path, I think, than Abbot Vonier's humble road of Christian discipleship.

Mark Judge

1

Christian Discipleship

For some people, the life of Christ here on earth lacks the element of originality. They can find nothing in the teaching and the power of Christ which could not have been found in the life of any other person of eminent sanctity. According to such interpreters of the career of the Son of Mary, He had no more influence for good, He was no nearer to men in the days of His mortality, than any other leader of outstanding quality.

Such opinions, of course, can only exist in those minds that have never studied the supreme spiritual problem of Christian discipleship. Christ gathered round Himself disciples; those disciples, in their turn, were commissioned to gather disciples not round themselves but round Christ, and so *in indefinitum*. Christianity is essentially discipleship of Christ and its deep originality lies therein. "In this is My Father glorified: that you bring forth very much fruit and become My disciples."[1] Christian fruitfulness and Christian discipleship represent God's success

1

amongst men. In the measure in which these two qualities take hold of the children of men the glory of the Father becomes more and more radiant on this earth.

Almost without exception Jesus Christ speaks of His followers as His disciples. The Evangelists, who wrote down what they had seen and heard, almost invariably make use of the term "disciple," it is only rarely that they give the name of "Apostle" to the Twelve. Before all things and above all things they are disciples. Later on, in the Acts, the converts are always described as disciples; and apostolic men like Timothy are given that name though it is not applied to the Apostles themselves. Saint Luke, the author of the Acts, notes the time when another title began to be bestowed on the believers in Christ: "And Barnabas went to Tarsus to seek Saul: whom, when he had found, he brought to Antioch. And they conversed there in the Church a whole year: and they taught a great multitude, so that at Antioch the disciples were first named Christians."[2]

No doubt it may be objected that other religious leaders and teachers of the time also called their followers disciples: there were, for example, the disciples of John the Baptist. Thus discipleship could not mean anything very new or original in the case of Christ. To this we reply that the originality we claim is to be found in this, that One of Christ's character should admit any human being into the relation of discipleship with Himself: the quality of the Master makes the newness of the discipleship. When the Son of God says that in this is the Father glorified, that we should become His disciples, He has indeed opened out for us infinite vistas and glorious possibilities, because a disciple may be anything from a mere tyro to a consummate doctor in the special wisdom of the Master, from a new convert to the confidant of all the secrets of the Leader. The term "Christian discipleship" stands for complete initiation into all the mysteries of Christ. Saint John the Divine ascribes all his exceptional privileges to the quality of this discipleship; because he is "the disciple whom Jesus loved" all things may come to him: "When Jesus therefore had seen His mother and the disciple standing whom He loved, He saith to His mother: Woman, behold thy son. After that, He saith to the disciple: Behold thy mother. And from that hour the disciple took her to his own."[3]

The first element in discipleship is knowledge of the Master: knowledge of doctrine is secondary, knowledge of the Person is paramount and constitutes the difference between a mere follower and a disciple. Christ expects that those who come to Him should know Him. Confidence in the Master is indeed an integral part of discipleship, but it does not primarily constitute it. The disciple is expected before all things to believe that the Master has knowledge, and in the case of Christ infinite knowledge is presupposed. The quality, then, of the disciple's knowledge is the clear vision that his Lord and Master is all-knowing. On one occasion Our Lord drew forth from Saint Peter a most explicit statement on this issue: "After this, many of His disciples went back and walked no more with Him. Then Jesus said to the twelve: Will you also go away? And Simon Peter answered Him: Lord, to whom shall we go? Thou hast the words of eternal life. And we have believed and have known that Thou art the Christ, the Son of God."[4]

The disciple of all times has one great task to perform, he must enter more and more into the secrets of the Master; he must be ready for any revelation his Leader may be preparing, any manifestation of His secret greatness. So Christian discipleship means being called to witness the miracle at the marriage feast of Cana and climbing Mount Tabor; being made to share the great Pasch of the Passion and watching in the Garden of Gethsemane; being met by the Risen Christ and being led by Him to the hilltop of the Ascension; being ordered to the Upper Room where the Spirit is to manifest Himself and being a partaker in a thousand other things, one more marvelous than the other. Who cannot see at a glance that Christian discipleship has no equal on earth nor rival in history? If the Christian were not a disciple he would be a very different being, spiritually, from what he is. His rank would be that of one who is a learner in a school, whereas actually he ought to be one whom Christ wants to follow Him wherever He goes, so that no aspect of His life is unknown to the disciple.

This element of knowledge, this comprehension of the very essence of Christ, profoundly differentiates the Christian from all other good men. This peculiarity could be summed up thus: it matters little to the Christian what he is himself, what other men are, what things in general are; but it matters intensely to him what Christ is, what men think of Him, what His prerogatives are. This is true discipleship, a passionate interest in the status of the Master, so that for one iota the disciple will fight unto death, if by that little the Master's dogmatic position is diminished, if it should imply that instead of being the equal of God He is only similar to God. Disciples have, indeed, no interest of their own, they have no doctrine of their own, no cause of their own, but the Master's position is everything to them.

This, then, is the peculiar characteristic of the Christian, precisely because he is a *discipulus*, he is a passionate dogmatist; indeed, the very best definition of the opposite of Christian discipleship would be "religion without dogma." What is the merit of following one who has no doctrines or whose doctrines are of no consequence? Certainly such followers could not aspire to be disciples though they might be soldiers or slaves. And so the *Christianus discipulus* has a very pronounced sensitiveness with regard to Christ's dogmatic value in the world, and to him a religious war would be more acceptable than religious indifference. He cannot understand morality except in its relation to the Master, for to him all ethics are love of that Master, loyalty to Him, obedience to His commandments and perseverance in His service. The behavior of a Christian is essentially that of a disciple, not of a philosopher, and many calls come to him which have their origin, not in human morality, but in discipleship: "If any man come to Me, and hate not his father and mother and wife and children and brethren and sisters, yea and his own life also, he cannot be My disciple. And whosoever doth not carry his cross and come after Me cannot be My disciple."[5]

It is a ludicrous pretension on the part of any one to start building a tower without first having reckoned the cost. Any man so doing is sure to be the object of public ridicule and people will say of him: "This man began to build and was not able to finish."[6] More serious still would be the plight of a king who was rash enough to declare war upon another sovereign who had double the military force. His humiliation must be great when things become grave and critical: "Or else, while the other is yet afar off, sending an embassy, he desireth conditions of peace."[7] Such preposterous actions are not more evident signs of lack of prudence than would be the attitude of the man who claims Christian discipleship and shuns abnegation: "So likewise every one of you that doth not renounce all that he possesseth cannot be My disciple."[8]

Declarations so solemn, fortified with some of the most striking metaphors of the Gospels, have led students of Christian spirituality to ask the question whether discipleship is meant for all who profess faith in Christ, or only for a select few; whether, in other words, discipleship is not a higher form of Christianity, in which the majority even of those who are baptized in Christ have no share, so that the person whom we call the ordinary Christian is a Christian without being truly a disciple. But it is obviously against the whole character of Christianity to admit of such a dilution of spiritual labor. Everyone who belongs to Christ, or desires to belong to Him, may be asked to have the readiness and the thoroughness here described, and a failure to renounce may often mean apostasy. Every Christian is radically prepared for martyrdom; it is implied in the state of grace in which he lives. He must lay down his life rather than renounce Christ or a single truth of the Christian faith. Nothing could show more clearly that true Christianity can only be interpreted in terms of discipleship than this principle of heroism universally accepted amongst its followers, that it is better to lose all things and even life itself than to doubt the validity of one single word uttered by Christ.

The future of Christ's Kingdom, even in its external setting, is described as a similarity of conditions shared by the Master and the disciple: "The disciple is not above the master, nor the servant above his lord. It is enough for the disciple that he be as his master, and the servant as his lord. If they have called the good-man of the house Beelzebub, how much more them of his household."[9]

At all periods of human history it is indispensable for Christians to remember that law of similarity. We are not asked to make of Christ's cause an unassailable triumph; we are not sent forth as soldiers to fight victorious battles that will establish the supremacy of the Son of God; any such metaphor, if pressed too far, would give a wrong conception of our mission in the Church. We are essentially disciples, whose glory it is to resemble our Master, to remember all He has said and done, to tell the world of it whenever we have a chance, to treasure His memory amongst ourselves if outsiders refuse to listen to us, but above all, to consider a perfect resemblance to Him as the highest goal of our aspirations.

So there is in all true Christianity a most persevering memory of the life of Christ, besides that keen fidelity to His doctrine. We treasure every one of His words and gestures, every act of His life, every detail of His death, as narrated by the Evangelists. The Apostles showed their discipleship in this, that they never tired of repeating the story of their Master as they carried on their great work of evangelizing the world. Memory as well as knowledge is an integral part of discipleship. In Christianity this memory of Christ has been erected into a memorial, a living monument, a mystery of remembrance—the Holy Eucharist. Discipleship is indeed intimately associated with this memorial of the Last Supper: "And taking bread, He gave thanks and brake and gave to them, saying: This is My Body, which is given for you. Do this for a commemoration of Me."[10]

In discipleship we have given to us the greatness as well as the limitation of our Christian hopes. We may hope for everything that is in Christ; we may hope to do the works which He did, and, as He says, even greater ones. No true Master has ever begrudged his faithful disciple a full share in his own powers. The least thing we do, the least thing that is done for us, at once acquires divine proportions, because we are disciples: "He that receiveth you receiveth Me: and he that receiveth Me receiveth Him that sent Me."[11] "And whosoever shall give to drink to one of these little ones a cup of cold water only in the name of a disciple, amen, I say to you, he shall not lose his reward."[12] But in discipleship we have also put before us our own limitations. It must be enough for us to be like the Master. We are not called upon to do work that would replace the Cross of Christ with an anticipated triumph of Christ. Our greatest celebration is the commemoration of His Death, until He come in glory.

Discipleship with Christ receives its consummation in the Paraclete, the Spirit of truth. It will be the mission of the Holy Spirit to complete the initiation, to put the coping-stone on the edifice of education in the mystery of Christ. Far from making discipleship superfluous, the Spirit puts the final touches to it, for Christ clearly proclaims that He did not do the whole work in His own lifetime.

A simple juxtaposition of Our Lord's utterances will be more impressive than any commentary for bringing home the radical dependence of every Christian disciple on the Trinity Itself.

> These things have I spoken to you, abiding with you. But the Paraclete, the Holy Spirit, whom the Father will send in My name, He will teach you all things and bring all things to your mind, whatsoever I shall have said to you.[13]

> But when the Paraclete cometh, whom I will send you from the Father, the Spirit of truth, who proceedeth from the Father, He shall give testimony of Me. And you shall give testimony, because you are with Me from the beginning.[14]

> I have yet many things to say to you: but you cannot bear them now. But when He, the Spirit of truth, is come, He will teach you all truth. For He shall not speak of Himself: but what things soever He shall hear, He shall speak. And the things that are to come, He shall show you. He shall glorify Me: because He shall receive of Mine and shall show it to you. All things whatsoever the Father hath are Mine. Therefore I said that He shall receive of Mine and show it to you.[15]

2

CHRISTIANUS SANCTIFICATUS

Christian Sanctification

Sanctity here on earth becomes formidable chiefly when it is attacked. We take many things for granted, we insert them into the daily round of our life without any tremor. But if a man be found who commits a profanation, such a one is considered by us all as a monster. In him the saying of Saint Paul becomes alarmingly manifest: "But if any man violate the temple of God, him shall God destroy."[16] We expect heavenly vengeance to fall upon that sacrilegious person.

Now this indignation springs from a very special characteristic of the Christian: he is a sanctified being. He has the sense, the genius, of sanctity. This gift he carries about him wherever he goes though he is mostly unconscious of it. It is not an impediment to his ordinary human life; he is not like one who walks as if he had a precious but fragile burden balanced on his head. His whole constitution is holy, and for this reason he is not aware of it in normal life. But let there be a profanation, of whatever kind, it will be like an arrow in his flesh. If the profanation be a vile sin committed by himself, the sense of violated sanctity will be all the more merciless.

Sanctity is not primarily action; it is above all things a quality. We might call it a static quality. Action is holy or unholy according as it is either in conformity with or a departure from an unchanging quality that imposes itself upon man's consciousness; every deed that is either holy or unholy resolves itself into the concepts of worthiness or unworthiness. A good man acts in a manner worthy of the state, of the quality that is his; or he behaves in a fashion that is entirely unworthy of himself. Truly, there could be no sin unless there were in us some initial worth which, in our perverted state, we tread under foot. If we were irremediably low and incurably degraded we could no more be guilty of moral transgression than the basest among the beasts, for we should be moving in conformity with our nature; such blind impulse could not be reckoned as guilt.

The deeds of the saints, when viewed in this clear light, show forth in their full splendor because they conform to the grace that is in them, for grace is essentially a quality of beauty. All sin, indeed, is a falling away from beauty, from holiness. Even when we say that a good man acquires holiness through a long exercise of virtue we mean, in strict theology, nothing else than a progressive worthiness; every day he becomes worthier and worthier of his calling:

> We are bound to give thanks always to God for you, brethren, as it is fitting, because your faith groweth exceedingly and the charity of every one of you towards each other aboundeth. So that we ourselves also glory in you in the churches of God, for your patience and faith, and in all your persecutions and tribulations: which you endure. For an example of the just judgment of God, that you may be counted worthy of the kingdom of God, for which also you suffer.[17]

With an astonishing majesty of emphasis Christ reduces the practice of highest self-abnegation to this simple formula of worthiness and unworthiness, but the Holy One who becomes the discriminator between good and evil is Himself: "He that taketh not up his cross and followeth Me is not worthy of Me."[18]

There is a whole world of spiritual wisdom in presenting action as the expression of worth. Fundamentally this attitude means that the tree is before the fruit; in other words, that the divine is among us before we are aware of its nearness, and that all progress consists in an increasing realization of its abiding presence in us. We are never asked to make great leaps in the spiritual life, as if we must jump a chasm from darkness into light. The flame is in our very soul, though we may be blind to it. "But the justice which is of faith, speaketh thus: Say not in thy heart: *Who shall ascend into heaven?* That is, to bring Christ down. *Or who shall descend into the deep?* That is, to bring up Christ again from the dead. But what saith the scripture? *The word is nigh thee, even in thy mouth, and in thy heart.* This is the word of faith, which we preach."[19]

It is more than Dantesque poetry, it is exact Catholic theology, to describe the fallen spirits, the devils, as being unceasingly in quest of places from which all holiness is banished, if such can be found; because Satan and his angels cannot dwell in holiness, just as they cannot stand in truth: "When an unclean spirit is gone out of a man, he walketh through dry places seeking rest and findeth none."[20] Even the Arabian deserts offer the apostate angel no comfort, for in them also are to be found regions of holiness and the atmosphere of sanctity. Is there a better place for prayer than the desert at sunset, with the glory of God made almost palpable? Nature is full of holiness, and everywhere the unclean spirit is out of touch with its real life. Rest has become impossible for him; the earth's surface burns the sole of his foot. Where will he go? "Then he saith: I will return unto my house from whence

I came out."[21] This is Christ's mighty poetry of the power of holiness. Even the desert becomes unbearable for Satan, the essentially unclean. A sinful conscience in man is his only chance of repose: "And they enter in and dwell there: and the last state of that man is made worse than the first."[22]

The task of historians would be greatly simplified were they to take to heart this revelation, made by the all-seeing Son of God, of the true movement of things—an innumerable host of unclean spirits finding it impossible to rest unless men's hearts be soiled by iniquity. The periodical desecration or profanation of vast Christian lands becomes as simple in this explanation as the advance of a Napoleonic army. Satan wants to find rest, so he must destroy, if he can, every stronghold of holiness, be it a church spire, be it a crucifix by the wayside, a convent, a school of Christian truth, or a conscience that is in the grace of God. With such things confronting him on all sides Satan cannot rest. To demolish sanctity in all its manifestations is as much a necessity for him as it is for an invader to destroy the strongholds of the legitimate occupants of a territory.

There is in Christ's epic presentment of the maneuvers of the unclean spirits a feature that may well make us pause.

The Son of God really foretells that saddest of all human eventualities, the apostasy of those whose soul had been cleansed of all sin, "empty, swept and garnished." There is prophesied a direct, subtly-planned and powerful attack on well-established sanctity, which, alas, is successful: "Then he goeth and taketh with him seven other spirits more wicked than himself: and they enter in and dwell there."[23] Might we not place these words as an introduction to many of the voluminous "Histories of Europe" which give the high-sounding title of "march of civilization" to results which, to the eyes of the believer, must be attributed to the marches and countermarches of an army that seeks rest and cannot find it in a Christian atmosphere?

Christianity started as an immense, nay, as an infinite hallowing of mankind. Is it not the whole meaning of the Incarnation that the Word should dwell among us full of grace and truth? Everyone brought into contact with that "Holy Thing," as the Offspring of Mary is called in the Gospel of Saint Luke,[24] is holy, as a sacred vessel is holy. The holiness into which Christian baptism admits the faithful is the commonplace of all the preachers of the Apostolic and Patristic age: "But you are washed: but you are sanctified: but you are justified: in the name of Our Lord Jesus Christ and the Spirit of our God."[25] Even with us the irresistible attraction of the little ones who are baptized in Christ and who believe in Him is a favorite topic, and it is not a sentimental illusion.

But let us beware lest we overlook the innate sanctification of all the sons of the Church, however rough the course of their mortal careers may be. Like pure gold, the Christian hallowing has a wonderful resistant quality; it can stand an immense amount of wear and tear. Satan has to fight hard, according to Christ's description, if he is to dwell at ease in a milieu that was at one time Christian. The reason of this durability is obvious: Christian sanctification is the act of God, not the act of man. When anything has been hallowed by the Spirit, God has appropriated that sanctified being and has made it His own. The efforts of the unclean spirits to render common that which once has been hallowed are truly gigantic. When, for instance, we come across the sad ruins of some ancient religious house in England, destroyed, debased, almost erased if not worse, we may well ponder on the immensity of evil-doing that was necessary to bring about such a disaster. On the physical side of things the proud temple of God has become the abode of unclean creatures if, indeed, there are any remnants at all. On the moral side a whole people's imagination is filled with impure calumnies and fantastic misrepresentations of the lives of those who dwelt in the ancient homes of sanctity.

The power which the Catholic Church possesses to hallow is truly prodigious; nor does the Church make any secret of it, she proclaims it before the whole world. She carries out this special mission of hers in a superb fashion, as the queen of the spiritual world. The dedication of a church is the divinely inspired counter-stroke to that activity of the unclean spirit of which Christ in the Gospel has given us such a vivid picture. The Church makes an assault on the finished material building; she enters into it in glory and in grace; and she bids her children follow her and find rest for their souls in a house now entirely given up to sanctity.

3

The Light of Christ

No one can fail to be impressed by man's resourcefulness in his efforts to turn the hours of night into hours of work and industry. In all ages of human activity light has been a guide in the obscurity of night. Man has always navigated his ships across the seas by the light of the stars, and he has found security in his journeys over desert wastes in the infinitesimal glimmer of distant constellations. We men of the feverish days of modern inventions have endless cause to marvel at the power light has to make our most dangerous venture more secure. Need one mention instances? The journey of an express train guided along its track at night by signals of light fills one with wonder. Daylight is indeed one of God's greatest blessings and a source of unceasing gladness; but what shall we say of the light that shines in darkness, of its helpfulness, of its power, of its reliability?

Christians are familiar with the great declaration of their Lord and Master: "I am the Light of the world." Scriptural utterances concerning this most blessed attribute of Christ, lightsomeness, are so numerous as to constitute a theology in themselves.

But considering the present phase of the Church's life, her period of militancy, we may legitimately ask in what way is Christ a light to us. Is He our light as the stars at night, as a lighthouse in the gloom of a winter's night at sea?

Saint John the Evangelist declares the Word Incarnate to be "Light that shineth in darkness," not in full and unchecked noon-day light. In Himself, of course, Christ is all light; He dwells in light; one day, in the glories of eternity, He will be light to all the elect in the Kingdom of the Father: "The city hath no need of the sun, nor of the moon, to shine in it. For the glory of God hath enlightened it: and the Lamb is the lamp thereof."[26]

But here on earth, while the troubles of the Church last, Christ is a light shining in darkness. Night is not ended, but hangs over us, heavy, somber and full of lurking dangers. But one thing Christ does—and this is His supreme claim when He says that He is the Light of the world—He makes possible every holy venture and activity by the help of His gracious light. Wherever you go, whatever you do in this world, you can walk and work by the light that is Christ. We are sure of our road, even though it be not broad daylight; if He is our guide we have always sufficient light for our journey.

It is in this way that we must think of Christ as the Light of the world until the great day of eternity dawns. It is not the will of the Father that darkness be entirely dissipated, that there be no night. But the Father has given us a Light that shines in darkness and illumines every man that walks upon the earth. We need not err, for the signals of that light are manifest beyond doubt.

It is, of course, true that many a privileged soul, even in this life, finds in Christ more than a guiding star. By His sweet presence in the heart of the mystic the glories of heaven seem to have descended to earth. Such men can say with Saint Paul: "For God, who commanded the light to shine out of darkness, hath shined in our hearts, to give the light of the knowledge of the glory of God, in the face of Christ Jesus."[27] But even at that height of illumination we know that we walk not by vision, but by faith. Our Christ will always be a light that shines in darkness.

The light of Christ is not only a guide to our steps, it is also a revealer of secrets. Through its power we see things as they are. The light of Christ is therefore a thing of stern reality as well as of comfort. For this is the characteristic of true Christian illumination, that the mind of man has the courage to look at the great truths and facts of divine justice and sanctity. Herein we find the difference between Christian illumination and false illuminism. The *illuminati* of all ages live in a fool's paradise, deluding themselves into the vision of a very one-sided presentment of the mystery of Christ. Now true Christian vision takes in not only the glorious and consoling facts, but likewise the hard realities of the world. The Christian sees sin and its punishment in proper perspective; he traces the hand of God in events that are unfavorable and painful; he has the genius to see the opportunity for grace and repentance where the heathen perceives nothing but confusion and disaster. Above all, in the light of Christ, he sees the distant goal, the end towards which all things move, and his vision is not held by nearer objects, but travels straight to that point where all things meet in the will and wisdom of God.

In our daily contact with the world and worldlings we are often baffled by what we instinctively feel to be an incredible shortsightedness. With our truly Catholic habit of visualizing the totality of things, we can hardly understand why people should boggle at small side issues. When we see sin and scandal, we at once look ahead to the acts of penance and reparation; when we have to contemplate failure in life, we think at once of possible future triumphs arising from that very failure. At no time is the present event our whole object of vision. We become good readers of history; with one sweep of intuition we embrace vast periods of Christian activity and we see everywhere the victories of Christ's grace in the midst of most unfavorable human circumstances. We have an eye tor the presence and snares of Satan in the world. In the words of Saint Paul: "We are not ignorant of his devices."[28]

For the splendor that is Christ's is a divine beam of whitest light cast on a real world, not a fanciful ideal world; a world of flesh and blood, of sin and justice, of angels and demons, of things beautiful and ugly. The light that illumines us, powerful as it is, does not blind us, but it has a wonderful way of showing to us life as it is in very truth.

Through the light of Christ we know that we are in a world of darkness; we have become expert discerners of darkness and the works of darkness. Were it not for that steady, unchanging light we might love the darkness, we might grow so accustomed to it as to take it for our natural element: "For you were heretofore darkness, but now light in the Lord. Walk then as children of the light."[29]

Such words as these bring home to our minds the state of spiritual benightedness which is man's natural condition. He will not be even conscious of his miserable predicament until the light of Christ pierce the darkness for him. His natural light, his reason, will become to him a further cause of blindness, it will even become darkness instead of a light: "If the light that is in thee be darkness: the darkness itself how great shall it be."[30] Discrimination between light and darkness is the special gift of the mind illumined by Christ.

We do not know how we came to be endowed with such faculty of vision. If we are converts we may remember the first moment of spiritual enlightenment, like Saint Paul when "there fell from his eyes as it were scales and he received his sight."[31] Before that hour struck we simply could not see. If, on the other hand, no such change was needed, if we have always enjoyed our spiritual sight, we still marvel at this difference between us and the blind world around.

It may be said in very truth that when Christ declared Himself to be the light of the world He put forth His greatest claim, with the exception, of course, of His claim to Divinity itself. He laid claim to the power of revealing the hidden things of darkness, of making manifest the counsels of man's hearts, of never leaving any one in doubt and perplexity even in the most prolonged periods of obscurity, if man be willing to look upon Him the Light of Life.

Physical light is the oldest symbol of Christ amongst Christians; not the blazing glare of a beacon, but the steady gleam of the oil lamp and the wax taper. It is a light shining in darkness, the luminous flicker of a lamp at the end of a long obscure gallery in the catacombs, or the tiny flame of a candle on an altar at the end of a dim aisle in a great cathedral. The gloom of the encircling darkness is pierced by it as by a sword, though the shadows still remain. Such is Christ's presence among men. With great gladness of heart we ought to greet the burning candle on the altar where the Holy Sacrifice is being celebrated. Each little flame should be for us an act of faith. Small as the flicker of the blessed candle may be, it still represents an infinitude—the infinite distance between light and darkness, the infinite power that said: "Let there be light."

And that which happens on the altar while the little flame of the candle consumes the wax is something analogous. An apparently small act, a sacramental rite of bread and wine. But infinitude is there, the infinitude of Christ's words at the Consecration.

There is wonderful, perhaps unconscious, art in the Church's selection of light as the symbol of Christ, the small flickering gleam that has been in all times the illumination of the dwellings of the poor. It is a mocking challenge to the spirit of darkness, to Satan, who tries to turn himself into an angel of light. The coruscations of mendacity are opposed to the simplicity of truth. Christ has in Himself power to be light, not in one way only, but in an infinite number of ways. From the faint flicker of the light of faith in the human soul—symbolized by the burning candle or the sanctuary lamp—to the vision of God in heaven, what a spiritual journey! Yet it is the same Christ at every stage. When Simeon held the infant Christ in his arms there was no effulgence coming from those limbs except the sweet whiteness of His immaculate body; yet of that Child he sang: *Lumen ad revelationem Gentium*; *A light to the revelation of the Gentiles.* Of the same body we read that one day it will appear in the heavens like a flash of lightning, illuminating the whole creation and revealing all the secrets of the consciences of men: "For as lightning cometh out of the east and appeareth even unto the west: so shall also the coming of the Son of Man be. Wheresoever the body shall be, there shall the eagles also be gathered together."[32]

4

The Indwelling Spirit in the Christian

The greatest of all the endowments of the Christian Church is the Holy Spirit. The Church is the House of the Spirit, the home of the Spirit; the Spirit dwells in the Church as He dwells nowhere else. It is of greatest importance in our analysis of the Christian man to give to the Spirit His proper place in the making of that supremely specialized being, the human person regenerated in Christ.

The Spirit that enters into the formation of the Christian is, by His very nature, an exclusive Spirit who is not to be found elsewhere in the same way as in the Christian soul. He is the Spirit of truth who is in the disciples of Christ, though the world cannot know or receive Him: "The spirit of truth, whom the world cannot receive, because it seeth Him not, nor knoweth Him. But you shall know Him; because He shall abide with you and shall be in you."[33] This is what we mean when we say that Christianity is entirely supernatural. It is a supremely specialized religion because

21

it is made up of gifts whose very existence, not to say whose worth, is known only to those who possess them. The Spirit that abides with the Christian is not a communicable privilege; there are no manifestations of that Spirit except in Christian life; He cannot be imitated; He cannot be simulated. There is no intermediary stage between the spiritual and the non-spiritual, they are two classes completely apart. The Spirit is something as original in the composition of the Christian economy of life as the Eucharist, as supernatural charity.

We come then at once to the question of the mystery of the first Pentecost. What was the gift bestowed on the Church that day? That an entirely new gift came to the Church is evident from the whole genius of the New Testament. It would not be enough to say that the Holy Spirit was given on Pentecost in a fuller measure than had been the case before. No, the descent of the Spirit which took place ten days after the Lord's Ascension was a thing unique in the history of the world, as unique as the Last Supper, as unique as Christ's death on Calvary. The Spirit had not been given before, but was bestowed in that ever-blessed hour; the ninth hour of the fiftieth day after the Easter of the Redemption.

The Holy Spirit had dealings with saintly men from the very beginning. Of Him it is said in the Creed that He had spoken through the mouth of the Prophets: *Qui locutus est per Prophetas*; in fact, there could be no holiness of any kind without the Spirit of God. Yet the Pentecost of the New Testament is an immense thing, an entirely new thing, and the Spirit is with us in a way not known to the Prophets and Kings who had a desire to see what we see, but did not see it; who had a desire to hear what we hear, but did not hear it. It is not too much to say that the presence of the Spirit in the Church of Christ since Pentecost is as new as is the presence of the Son of God since the Incarnation. God was always with man, God had walked with man, God had made of man His friend, yet it cannot be said that God had become man or that He dwelt among men in the way in which He now abides among us, since those things were accomplished in Mary which had been foretold to her by the angel. The Incarnation is an entirely new way for God to be with man; the abiding of the Paraclete in the New Testament belongs to the same plane of reality; it is as new, as original, as the birth of the Word in time. It would not be allowable to call it the incarnation of the Third Person of the Trinity, because the Spirit did not take flesh as the Word took flesh. What I say is this, that the advent of the Paraclete is of the same kind as the coming of the Son of God; in both instances there is a true *descensus de coelo*, a true coming down from heaven, as had not been before. In what way this new advent differs so profoundly from the whisperings of the Spirit in the ancient world before Christ, theologians have tried to understand and explain; but they are faced with as great a mystery as the mystery of the Incarnation. As it is God's secret how the Son of God became man, so it is His secret how the Spirit of God dwells in man; but in both of these instances it is literally true that a divine Person and no one else has been seen and has conversed with man here on earth.

I could repeat all that has been written by theologians in order to explain the meaning of this new abiding of the Paraclete. But the wisest of them confess that all their words are but childish babbling. They state, for instance, that through the coming of the Holy Spirit the Christian soul has a special and exclusive orientation towards the Third Person of the Trinity. With Saint Paul they say that we are sealed in the Holy Spirit as we are sealed with the sign of Christ in Baptism. This is a clear insinuation that the Paraclete is as much to us as the Word Incarnate. But I think it is sufficient for all purposes of Christian theology to affirm this parity between the advent of the Son of God and the descent of the Holy Spirit, though the one came taking flesh while the other took, as it were, the whole Church to Himself.

In this connection the book of the Acts of the Apostles gains immensely in theological importance, because it is truly the Gospel of the Holy Spirit, as the writings of the four Evangelists are the Gospel of the Incarnate God. In the Acts we have the history of the manifestation of the Spirit, and there is no reason why the Acts should not be considered as depicting the normal state of the Church of Christ. We know that most of the doctrine of the Spirit, as enunciated by Christ, has been written down by Saint John. The Acts, on the other hand, have for their author Saint Luke, who was not one of the Twelve who heard Christ's words concerning the Spirit, utterances that fill the interval between the mystical sacrifice of the Last Supper and the pouring out of His Blood in the Passion. Yet there is such a complete harmony between the realization of the promise of the Spirit in the early Church as described in the Acts, and the promise itself as found in the Gospel of Saint John, that one could almost feel tempted to see in Saint John the inspirer of Saint Luke. Nothing could be easier for my reader than to verify for himself this all-pervading belief in the Spirit in the early Church as shown in Saint Luke's narrative. The Spirit has become truly that "other Paraclete," that other companion, that other friend abiding with them after Christ's departure: "I will ask the Father: and He shall give you another Paraclete, that He may abide with you forever."[34]

The assurance of the Son of God that He would not leave the Apostles orphans has been verified in a most striking fashion, for if there is one note completely absent in the mentality of the early Church it is the feeling of loneliness and bereavement; there is a fullness of life, there is a spiritual contentment, there is an assurance of outlook which was never surpassed in the days when Christ Himself walked with His Apostles and worked before their eyes wonders and miracles that filled them with astonishment. The Acts are the best explanation of that almost bewildering statement of Christ: "I tell you the truth: it is expedient to you that I go. For if I go not, the Paraclete will not come to you: but if I go I will send Him to you."[35]

When we read the Acts of the Apostles we find everywhere a spiritual maturity, nay, even a boldness and daring which would not be possible if there were present a leader in human form whose word would be supreme law. The Apostles themselves now speak as guides and lawgivers: "For it has seemed good to the Holy Spirit and to us to lay no further burden than these necessary things."[36] The Apostles here reasoned in the full consciousness of their power, a consciousness which, humanly speaking, would not have been possible with the overshadowing personality of Christ still visibly present among them.

May it not be said that Christ's words just related, as to the necessity of His departure, contain the most beautiful and most interesting problem of spiritual psychology? The removal of the visible, the personal presence of the Leader, far from diminishing the influence of that Leader, brings Him out before man in His full proportions. He is seen by the eye of the mind as He has never been seen before. He becomes active in a much more universal way, nay, He seems to be more present than when the eye of the flesh could perceive Him. "Behold I see the heavens opened and the Son of Man standing at the right hand of God."[37] This vision of Stephen in the power of the Spirit is truly the Christian vision all the world over.

Christ was emphatic in His declaration that His departure from this earth would not only be no loss, but would be a positive gain. Such is certainly the impression made on us when we read the Acts of the Apostles. "He shall glorify Me: because He shall receive of mine and shall show it to you."[38] This alone would profoundly differentiate the abiding of the Paraclete in the Christian from those breathings of the Spirit which inspired the Prophets of old. The Spirit who came down at Pentecost is essentially the Spirit of Jesus, the Spirit through whom Mary conceived, and who gives us Christ in a new and more intimate way.

The coming of the Spirit is not a superseding of Christ. Far be it from us even to hint at such misstatement of so high a mystery.

It is not even a succession of one power following upon another, as if Christ had done His share in the redemption of man and gone back to the Father, leaving the Spirit to take up the work. The Spirit that descended comes with all the aroma of the Incarnation.

There is no discontinuity, there is not even succession, but there is inwardness taking the place of outwardness. The Spirit who was in Christ all along, now rules the Church, and rules it with an energy and efficiency that make Him into something that is again almost palpable and outward, for if there is a characteristic of that Epiphany of the Spirit which began at Pentecost it is this, that He acts and speaks manifestly and that His works are visible.

In some instances His presence is even more manifest than the outward sacrament of water. When Peter spoke the words of the Gospel to Cornelius and his house,

> the Holy Spirit fell on all them that heard the word. And the faithful of the circumcision, who came with Peter, were astonished for that the grace of the Holy Spirit was poured out upon the Gentiles also. For they heard them speaking with tongues and magnifying God. Then Peter answered: Can any man forbid water, that these should not be baptized, who have received the Holy Spirit, as well as we? And he commanded them to be baptized in the name of the Lord Jesus Christ.[39]

May it not truly be said that in this characteristic we have one of the profoundest originalities of Christianity, a differentiation so far-reaching that it makes all comparison with other religions impossible. The one and the same dispensation can be expressed in terms of flesh and blood and in terms of the Spirit, the work of Christ is the work of the Holy Spirit in all things that are the Church's sanctification. We do not say indeed, that the Holy Spirit redeemed the world, but we say very truly with Saint Paul that "Christ by the Holy Spirit offered Himself unspotted to God"[40] as the Victim of our Redemption.

It is the Holy Spirit who saves the life of Christ from being merely an historical event. Through the Spirit all things that Christ did and said are permanently with us. Through the Spirit we have the Eucharist, not in the sense of the Protestant, who makes of the mystery of the Last Supper an exclusively spiritual thing, by which, in reality, he means an exclusively mental thing; but in the sense in which He is at the root of the Incarnation itself, for it is through the power of the Spirit that bread is changed into Christ's Body and wine is changed into Christ's Blood.

There is perceptible amongst our moderns a worship of the Spirit which makes of Him, not another Paraclete who receives from Christ and announces Him to us, but a new power succeeding the personal Christ and completely replacing Him. Such, of course, is not the true Christian cult of the Holy Spirit. Through the Spirit the personal Christ becomes present: our worship of the Spirit is unique in this sense that He brings Jesus so near us.

One cannot help being impressed by the extremely realistic presentment of the gift of the Spirit in Apostolic literature; the Christian can no longer do anything without his action being a reaction on the Spirit. If he is false in his dealings with the Church he is said to lie to the Holy Spirit; the gifts of the Spirit are so perceptible that Simon, the converted magician, offers money in exchange for them; the infidelities of the Christian heart are represented as a saddening of the Spirit; nay, the Christian has even the terrible power of extinguishing the Spirit in his soul, as a lamp is extinguished in a room. The Apostles go forth to give the Spirit to men to whom the deacons had given Baptism; and certain men are known through the more abundant measure of the Spirit that is in them, as others are known through their learning and eloquence. The possession of the Spirit is so evident that it renders a man fit for a higher office in the Church: "Wherefore, brethren, look ye out among you seven men of good reputation, full of the Holy Spirit and wisdom, whom we may appoint over this business."[41]

The Holy Spirit orders the life of the early Christians, sending men out to special missions, and in all things behaving with the supreme authority of the Master of the house. In very truth the *Christianus spiritualis*, as seen in the Apostolic days, is the House of the Spirit.

5

The Christian at Prayer

Prayer has been man's unceasing cry to God. It is the most universal evidence that there is in him something higher than his natural life. Man has supplicated and thanked God in every known tongue from the beginning of time.

Prayer is not an act exclusively Christian. The Jews prayed, the heathen prayed, long before the days of Christ. Yet Christian prayer was quite a new concept, which did not exist before Christ taught us "how to pray." He founded a prayer as He founded a Church; Christian prayer is His own original creation because it is unlike any other prayer. The only way in which it resembles the spontaneous cry to God which is found all the world over is in the fundamental element that it is addressed to God and not to man. In all other respects the Christian prayer is something original, something *sui generis*,[42] even as the Incarnation or Christ's resurrection or the Church or the Sacraments, for these are entirely new facts and were never known before the fullness of time.

"And it came to pass that as He was in a certain place praying, one of His disciples said to Him: Lord, teach us to pray, as John also taught his disciples."[43] The Apostles were familiar with the notion of prayer; what Jew was not? John, the holiest of them, had taught a most excellent form of prayer; would the great Master be behind John and other leaders of the spirit? Would not He also have a prayer worthy of His supreme claim? "And He said to them: When you pray, say: Father, hallowed be Thy name."[44]

Christ, then, had been appealed to for a great gift, and His answer was immediate, unreserved, most complete. In no other matter do we find Our Lord acceding so directly to a demand. He truly gave us a prayer as He gave us grace, as He gave us His Flesh to eat and His Blood to drink. It is *His* prayer, not merely "prayer" as already known; it is the prayer suited to that new condition in which men find themselves when admitted into companionship with Christ; henceforth it is as His disciples that they pray; the "Our Father" is given, not to all men, but to them; they alone can say it with truth and sincerity. It is an extremely important feature in the doctrine of Christian prayer—a feature, perhaps, not always attended to—that Christ gave this prayer to a definite group of men, who had a definite life and purpose. This prayer is, in a way, as exclusive in its purpose as are His Sacraments. It is for you, He says, thus to pray, as it is for you to eat My Flesh and drink My Blood. The prayer meets the needs of your society; not so much of you individually, as of you considered as My disciples. You pray, not your prayer, but the prayer of God's kingdom, the prayer of heaven.

That there is novelty in the Christian prayer is made clear by those other words of Our Lord to His disciples: "Hitherto, you have not asked anything in My name. Ask, and you shall receive; that your joy may be full."[45] Often had the Apostles prayed, they were good men, religious and pious; but a new prayer was given to them now, as a new commandment was given to them: "A new commandment I give unto you: That you love one another, as I have loved you, that you also love one another."[46] The Master bound them to that charity which binds together all those that are Christ's, and makes them into one body, one family of God.

So the new prayer is also a prayer of fellowship, a prayer in the name of the divine Leader, a prayer concerned with the interests of the King of souls, a prayer, not of individual, pious men, but a prayer of the people of Christ, of the army of God, a prayer as directly connected with the mystery of the Incarnation and with that of Christ's mystical Body, as the Eucharist itself. The Christian at prayer asks the Father, not in his own name but in the name of the Son of God: "Amen, amen, I say to you: if you ask the Father anything in My name, He will give it you."[47]

All this, of course, means much more than a mere mention of the name of Christ as a conclusion to our prayer. Prayer itself has been changed from the solitary cry of the distressed human heart into a great act of sacramental power, where there is no longer the lone effort of human supplication, but the music of the voice of the Son of God entering into the ears of the Father.

It is sad to see how very much neglected is this fundamental aspect of Christian prayer in many a well-meaning treatise written with the laudable aim of making us prayerful. Without being hypercritical, I may be allowed to say that very often the only prayer known to writers on this matter seems to be the personal prayer, supernatural of course, yet essentially individualistic and isolated. Such people seem to miss completely the all-important point that Our Lord has changed prayer from being an unsocial act; He has made it into the corporate act of the mystical Body of which He is the Head. Not only has He given us a fresh motive for hope in prayer, He has done more; He has made a new prayer, infallible, certain, unmistakable, like all the other things which

He has created in the supernatural order. The Spirit of prayer is essentially the same Spirit that animates the whole Body of the Church, and that Spirit never moves a soul except on concentric lines, that all should meet in the fullness of Christ. "Likewise, the Spirit also helpeth our infirmity. For, we know not what we should pray for as we ought: but the Spirit Himself asketh for us with unspeakable groanings. And He that searcheth the hearts knoweth what the Spirit desireth: because He asketh for the saints according to God. And we know that to them that love God all things work together unto good: to such as, according to His purpose, are called to be saints."[48]

"He asketh for the saints according to God" expresses in a few words that newness of life which Christ in His omnipotence has breathed into man's natural bent for prayer. The *disjuncta membra*[49] of the scattered pieties of the human race are united into one body, become a living organism, are given a heart to unite them all, to vivify them all; and in that heart there dwells the Holy Spirit Himself, and the longings of that heart are infinite, immense, otherworldly beyond comparison. "The Spirit Himself asketh for us with unspeakable groanings."

None of us is the object of the love of God in an exclusive fashion. None of us receives graces unconnected with the graces of other men; our very predestination implies a definite place in the temple of God of which we are the living stones. Were we given in this life the vision of our supernatural interdependencies with other souls who work out their salvation, great indeed would be our wonder. Of all the things of the Spirit prayer is the one which has the greatest power of communicability; it simply cannot be confined to the individual in its results. Prayer is a ray of sunshine which must illumine the whole countryside, as in spring we see a small rift in the clouds making a passage for the sunlight which will illuminate hills and dales far beyond the spot over which the clouds were rent.

True Christian prayer is usually in the plural. The divinely dictated prayer—the "Our Father"—is essentially the prayer of Christ's followers in their corporate capacity; the prayers of the Liturgy generally ignore the individual; many may pray for one person, as when we pray for the Pope, but no one ever prays alone, as if he were expected in the strength of his singlehanded wrestling with God to obtain the divine favor. It is true that in the secret of our chamber many of us use the first person singular in our supplication; perhaps we do it unconsciously, but let us be under no illusion, our prayer when most hidden and most personal is still a groaning of the Spirit who "asketh for the saints according to God." We pray with others because they also, perhaps at the very same moment, ask of God the things we ask.

The Christian prayer is quite infallible because of its universality of purpose; none of the demands of the "Our Father" are ever refused, because the Body of Christ, the People of God, are the direct objects of the divine favors for which it asks. Truly, the name of God is being constantly hallowed by His servants; the kingdom of heaven is manifested at every moment, the will of God finds its gracious accomplishment at all times in the world of souls sanctified in the grace of Christ. God feeds His people without ceasing, God forgives His people their trespasses, God preserves His people from temptations, and delivers them from evils as surely, as continuously, as the stars move in the firmament. Any Christian who says the Lord's Prayer does, in a way, a sacramental act that works with absolute certainty, because whatever he asks for is granted to the people to which he belongs.

It may be said that isolated prayer simply does not exist in Christianity: no Christian could pray in such wise as to obtain a thing from God which would have no reference to other Christians and which would not be of advantage to the other followers of Christ. It would mean an end to the life of the mystical Body of Christ if any of us could deal with God outside our fellowship with all other believers. No prayer of ours could ever be detrimental to someone else, as if it were diverting to ourselves graces and favors meant for other people. "God is rich unto all men that call upon Him"; no enrichment of the one brings impoverishment to the other, on the contrary, our spiritual wealth adds to the possessions of others. When Saint Paul says that he does not seek what is profitable to himself, but profitable to many, he not only gives us the quality of his own charity, but he really states a law of the spiritual life, which profits the whole mystical Body of Christ.

Many of our troubles about prayer would cease if we understood better this great truth that Christ's prayer is not of the one, but of the many; that in prayer we are an army arrayed in battle. We cry for victory, not for the individual soldier, but for the whole host. Is there anything more impressive than this theology of the Christian prayer? The last and the least of us has in himself the spirit and the genius of the whole mighty army of God; he knows that all is well with him if all is well with the immense host itself. He cries to God with millions of other fellow-combatants to be delivered from the snares of the enemy, to be led on to victory over evil, and he knows that the tremendous cry in which he joins penetrates to the throne of God. He is truly the *Christianus orans*, the Christian at prayer. He asks for things which embrace heaven and earth; he has at heart interests greater than the interests of the mightiest empire; he speaks to God of the fortunes of the kingdom of God as if they were the concerns of his own family. *Thy kingdom come, Thy will be done, on earth as it is in heaven*, who could ever pray thus except a Christian? Is it thinkable that a pious pagan, when speaking to his deity, more or less vague, would ask for anything except personal and temporal advantages? To ask God to manifest His own glory is a Christian intuition: it is only the Christian standing in prayer who can rise to such heights.

In our age of spiritual introversion and psychological preciousness, vocal prayer has become more or less the poor relation of what is called mental prayer. This slight is not justified. Vocal prayer, in the best Christian tradition, is the mass prayer, the corporate prayer, or better still the *vox sponsae*, the voice of the Bride of Christ; that voice which softened the heart of Saint Augustine when he heard it in the old basilica at Milan. To depreciate vocal prayer would be as truly uncatholic as to depreciate visible Church government and the external signs of grace we call the Sacraments.

Let us for a moment imagine a great congregation of English Catholics in one of our cathedrals, either actual or future, reciting in unison any of the Sunday collects with as much fervor as schoolchildren now pray to the Little Flower for fine weather on a picnic day. Suppose the collect which they are reciting so devoutly is that of the Third Sunday after Easter: "O God, who didst show the light of the truth unto those that go astray, that they may return into the way of righteousness; grant that all who are counted of the Christian faith may cast aside whatever is opposed to that name, and follow that which is fitting to it. Through Our Lord."

When such habits of prayer shall have taken possession of our good people then we shall be able to feel that something great has come to pass. And yet there were times when, doubtless, our present dream of the future was a daily occurrence among Christians. The Liturgy of the Church, as we have it now, was the "popular devotion" of an earlier age. The *Christianus orans* of those days is truly a classical figure in the history of spiritual things.

In this chapter I have used the term "prayer" with the same meaning as the old Latin verb *orare*; it is the prayer of intercession, of supplication, of thanksgiving, of praise; "I desire, therefore, first of all, that supplications, prayers, intercessions, and thanksgivings be made for all men."[50] For a long time now the word prayer has been used practically for the whole life of the spirit, from the laborious effort of the novice to conceive a good thought, to the ecstasy of the saint. As a consequence much stress has been laid, perhaps unconsciously, on the individualistic side of prayer, prayer being considered chiefly as the relation of the one soul with the One God; *Sola Soli* is a favorite maxim of much modern spirituality— "Alone with the Alone."

But it is evident that such exclusiveness ought not to be encouraged too far. Even if we take prayer in the enlarged modern sense, even if we take it to mean contemplation, ecstasy, union with God in every degree of nearness and spiritual purity of mind, the element of fellowship pervades it all. The supreme object of our contemplation is the mystery of Christ and of His Church. Now what is the mystery of Christ? "That the Gentiles should be fellow-heirs, and of the same body: and co-partners of His promise in Christ Jesus, by the gospel."[51] The nearer we come to God, the more we find God and His Christ in the company of the elect, "for by Him we have access both in one Spirit to the Father. Now therefore you are no more strangers and foreigners: but you are fellow-citizens with the saints and the domestics of God, built upon the foundation of the apostles and prophets, Jesus Christ Himself being the chief cornerstone."[52]

There is no more fruitful subject of daily meditation, for the tyro as well as for the veteran in the spiritual life, than the privileges which come to us through our fellowship with the other "saints," be they on earth, be they in heaven. Saint Paul seems to have made this the habitual subject of his own meditation: "Wherefore, I also, hearing of your faith that is in the Lord Jesus and of your love towards all the saints, cease not to give thanks for you, making commemoration of you in my prayers."[53]

6

The Christian at Sacrifice

The *Christianus orans*, the Christian at prayer, is indeed man at his best and noblest. But the Christian prayer has never been without a certain element of mysteriousness which soon forced itself upon the attention of the world. It was whispered among their pagan fellow-citizens that when the Christians came together to pray things were taking place that were graver than appeared on the surface; besides praying, the Christians were doing something, were performing mysterious and awful rites. The pagan world was aware of this in the first centuries, nor did the Christians seek to deny the fact. Why should they not have their own mysterious rites as other religions had theirs? The Christians were careful, of course, not to divulge the real nature of those acts and celebrations which were the true and solid center of their prayer.

We know that the mysterious element which forms the hidden kernel of the Christian prayer from the very beginning is the

Christian sacrifice. It there is the *Christianus orans*, the Christian at prayer, there is also the *Christianus sacrificans*, the Christian at sacrifice. In fact, in traditional Christianity the two attitudes are one and the same, or rather are so completely interwoven that the Christian prayer par excellence is found in the words and acts that prepare, constitute and complete the Christian sacrifice. The Christian sacrifice is the crest of the wave of the Christian prayer. The Christian himself is as much at home in the element of sacrifice as he is in the element of prayer.

Of all the religious acts of which man is capable, the act of sacrifice is the most simple and the most direct. There is a naturalness, a literalness of meaning in the act of sacrifice which man soon loses when he tries to commune with God in a more subjective and more abstract fashion. Complicated rites of a minor order may surround the act of sacrifice or the victim, but man has always understood that when he offers up a sacrifice he gives something to God, as when he gives his daughter away to the man who marries her. The marriage contract may develop into the most fantastic wedding festivities, with ceremonies full of meaning or meaningless, yet the fundamental fact remains, clear, simple and direct as the song of a bird, to be understood by everybody: "A man shall leave father and mother, and shall cleave to his wife: and they shall be two in one flesh."[54]

In sacrifice man goes to his God with a gift, an absolute gift, a gift to be bestowed without regret. If God gives back to him some part of it, or even the whole, the better for man; but the expectation of such return is only incidental to the gift which is the sacrifice. The circumstance that has contributed most towards the unchanging meaning and orthodoxy of the act of sacrifice is this, that sacrifice implies a definite victim or object to be given, to be selected for definite characteristics, to be offered up at a definite time, in a definite place, with acts and ceremonies exactly fixed by tradition. A man no more makes a mistake about his sacrifice than he does about his daughter in the matrimonial solemnity. It was with an enviable precision that the Israelite was told how to appease the Lord; the whole matter was truly so businesslike:

> The person that sweareth, and uttereth with his lips, that he would do either evil or good, and bindeth the same with an oath, and his word, and having forgotten it afterwards understandeth his offense. Let him do penance for his sin: and offer of the flocks an ewe lamb, or a she-goat, and the priest shall pray for him and his sin. But if he be not able to offer a beast, let him offer two turtles, or two young pigeons to the Lord, one for sin, and the other for a holocaust, and he shall give them to the priest: who shall offer the first for sin, and twist back the head of it to the little pinions, so that it stick to the neck, and be not altogether broken off. And of its blood he shall sprinkle the side of the altar: and whatsoever is left, he shall let it drop at the bottom thereof, because it is for sin. And the other he shall burn for a holocaust, as is wont to be done. And the priest shall pray for him, and for his sin, and it shall be forgiven him.[55]

More than with any other sacrifice, this clearness of purpose is the glorious privilege of the Christian sacrifice. The *Christianus sacrificans* goes to his temple with a purpose so definite that the very purity of his intention and object is to him a spiritual exhilaration. Let us look at him, at his faith, at his whole attitude, as he sallies forth from his everyday avocations to the sublime act of a divine sacrifice, great beyond all the sacrifices of other times and places. The Christian knows that the Son of God offered Himself a perfect holocaust, a sacrifice of infinite sweetness unto God. The death of Christ on the Cross is the one true Christian sacrifice. The Christian has heard Saint Paul's solemn declaration that Christ "hath delivered Himself for us, an oblation and a sacrifice to God for an odor of sweetness."[56] To be as "an odor of sweetness" has been the merit of every sacrifice from that of Noah onwards.

The Christian knows that Christ would not "offer Himself often, as the high priest entereth into the Holies every year with the blood of others."[57] Is it not the very heart of the Christian's hope that "Christ was offered once to exhaust the sins of many"?[58] The Christian conscience is, as it were, haunted by the memory of this great event, the death of God, the sacrifice of the Lamb of God, and its inexhaustible wealth of mercy. What, then, does the Christian go forth to see, having the memory of the sacrifice of the Son of God on Calvary? He still goes forth to see a sacrifice, to partake of a sacrifice, nay, to offer a sacrifice with as much clearness of purpose as if he had been bidden to pick out a lamb from his flock and bring it to the priest. For although the sacrifice of the Son of God cannot be repeated in the natural and terrible setting of the first Good Friday, it can be repeated, in all truth and all reality, *in mysterio, in sacramento.*

We shall see presently that the mystery and the sacrament, far from diminishing man's religion in the act of sacrifice, on the contrary enhance it. For the moment let us bear testimony to the universal historical fact that although the Christian sacrifice be *in mysterio, in sacramento*, the Christian steps up to the altar with as direct a purpose as if his sacrifice were a lamb from his flock, or as if, for the true Isaac, Christ—who cannot be immolated in His natural self any more—he were bidden, like Abraham, to offer up a ram. The circumstance that the new sacrifice, instead of being Christ in His natural self, is *in mysterio, in sacramento*, in nowise affects the intense realism of the sacrifice.

Let us follow the Latin Christian, a strong and most orthodox type of Christian if ever there was one; let us hear the sacrificial words that are uttered in his name by his priest. For to speak of the ordinary Catholic as a sacrificant is no excess of language. The faithful have their official priesthood whose powers and ministries they know well. But nothing would be more contrary to the very essence of the Christian priesthood than to separate it from the laity with an impassable gulf of privilege. The priest sacrifices essentially for the people, in the name of the people. In the sacrifice he is, as it were, the hands of the Christian people. "Brethren, pray that my sacrifice and yours may be acceptable to God the Father almighty"—*Orate, fratres, ut meum ac vestrum sacrificium*: an emphatic reminder of the part played by all who are present at the sacrifice.

> Receive, O holy Father, this spotless host, which I, Thine unworthy servant, do offer unto Thee, my God, living and true, for mine own countless sins, transgressions, and failings, and for all here present; as also for all faithful Christians, living or dead; that it may avail both me and them unto health for life everlasting.
>
> We offer unto Thee, O Lord, the chalice of salvation, beseeching Thee in thy mercy that it may rise up as a sweet savor before Thy divine majesty, for our salvation and for that of the whole world.
>
> Receive, O holy Trinity, this offering which we make to Thee in remembrance of the passion, resurrection and ascension of Our Lord Jesus Christ...
>
> May the Lord receive the sacrifice at thy hands to the praise and glory of His name, to our own benefit and to that of all His holy Church.[59]

There is no question here of a distant remembrance, of something merely imaginary. The words of the sacrificial offering can have only one meaning, the bread and the cup held in the hands of the priest are offered up to God as truly as was ever done in the Tabernacle of old, though with an immensely higher signification.

So far we have quoted the unchanging, the daily words of the sacrifice, ever old and ever new. But in the very midst of the sacrificial action there is what one might call a sudden inspiration, a prayer, often a series of prayers—the *Secreta*.[60] Innumerable are the testimonies contained in the *Secreta* of the Latin Mass in support of that astonishing literalness of the words of the Christian at his sacrifice. Let us hear him, for example, when he is in a more solemn mood, when he prays for his departed fellow-Christians.

> Receive, O Lord, we beseech Thee, the sacrifice which I offer up to Thee on behalf of the souls of my father and mother.

> Be merciful, O Lord, we beseech Thee, to the soul of Thy servant for which we offer up to Thee the sacrifice of praise.

> Graciously receive, O Lord, the victim which we offer up on behalf of the souls of Thy servants and handmaids and of all who sleep in Christ, whether in this place or elsewhere.

Man has always added to his sacrifice a prayer that it may be accepted by God; the Christian at sacrifice makes this invocation his own, repeating it in solemn fashion:

> In an humble spirit and a contrite heart may we be received by Thee, O Lord, and may our sacrifice so be offered up in Thy sight that it may be pleasing to Thee, O Lord God.

> Come, Thou who makest holy, almighty and everlasting God; and bless this sacrifice which is prepared for the glory of Thy holy name.

> Wherefore, O most merciful Father, we Thy suppliants do pray and beseech Thee through Jesus Christ, Thy Son, Our Lord, to receive and bless these gifts and offerings, this holy and unblemished sacrifice.

The Christian at sacrifice goes even so far as to crave for his sacrifice that approval which God bestowed on the sacrifice of His friends of old: "Vouchsafe to look upon [these gifts] with a countenance merciful and kind, and to receive them, as Thou was pleased to receive the gifts of Thy just servant Abel, and the sacrifice of our father Abraham, and that which Melchizedek Thy high priest offered up to Thee, a holy sacrifice and spotless victim."

Not of a distant victim, but of the holy things actually on the altar, the priest says in the plural, as the official delegate of the Christian people: "We Thy servants, as also Thy holy people... do offer unto Thy most excellent majesty of Thine own gifts bestowed upon us." Five times does the priest make the sign of the Cross over the *Oblata*, the elements on the altar, to signify that these things are indeed "a pure Host, a holy Bread, a Chalice of everlasting salvation." If ever there was a sacrificant who had his offering at hand, who beheld his victim with his own eyes, the Christian is that sacrificant. The words that signify unmistakable presence are multiplied in the sacrificial utterances of the Christian rite. The Latin demonstrative pronoun or adjective, is forced into service at every turn: *Hanc immaculatam Hostiam*; *Hujus aquae et vini mysterium*; *Benedic hoc sacrificium*; *Haec dona, haec munera, haec sancta sacrificia illibata*; *Hanc igitur oblationem servitutis nostrae*; *Jube haec perferri*; *Ex hac altaris participatione.*[61]

That the whole Christian sacrifice, whatever its nature, is there on the altar, is performed between given moments of ritual ceremonies, of that there can be no doubt. The hands of the priest cover it; with every kind of word and gesture he gives emphasis to it; and so evident is the presence of the Victim that the crowning act is the consuming of It. The eating and the sacrificing are of the same Flesh. The priest does not sacrifice a more recondite thing and eat a more present one. He eats that which he has sacrificed. Greater directness, greater presence, let us say greater palpability, no sacrifice could possess. To the Christian's sacrifice could be applied the phrase of Saint Paul concerning the word of faith: "Say not in thy heart: Who shall ascend into heaven? That is to bring Christ down; or who shall descend into the deep? That is, to bring Christ again from the dead. But what saith the scripture? The word is nigh thee, even in thy mouth and in thy heart. This is the word of faith, which we preach."[62]

The Christian is indeed the sincerest of all men who ever went up to God with gifts in their hands. But, as I have already said, he is a sacrificant of a higher type than were the Patriarchs of old. He sacrifices *in mysterio, in sacramento*. By this his dignity is much increased. What was mere dawn in the Patriarchs, in him is noontide sun. Nothing is more evident than the external, visible elements of his sacrifice. Bread and wine are given a glorious prominence; they are not hidden away, they are not thought to be too lowly or too unworthy for gifts to God; they are not brought in by stealth, as if their commonness were an obstacle to a higher presence. On the contrary, the bread and wine are made things of triumph at the Christian sacrifice. For a long time the Christian brought his own bread to the altar. From the earliest ages water has been mixed with the wine, as a sign—*per hujus aquae et vini mysterium*—of his participation in the mystery of Christ's Incarnation.

What then is a sacrificant *in mysterio, in sacramento*? The Canon of the Latin Mass reveals the wonderful privilege of such a man. After the most solemn rites of oblation, after having lifted the bread and wine before the face of God, the priest of the new dispensation is heard to utter a prayer, which no sacrificant of old ever dared to conceive: "This our offering, do Thou, O God, vouch-safe in all things to bless, consecrate, approve, make reasonable and acceptable, that it may become for us the Body and Blood of Thy most beloved Son, Our Lord Jesus Christ." *Ut nobis Corpus et Sanguis fiat dilectissimi Filii tui Domini nostri Jesu Christi.*

This indeed is to offer sacrifice in a mystery, in a sacrament: firstly, to do all the external acts of a natural, mortal sacrifice, as Melchizedek had done, as the Levites in the Temple had done; secondly, to have the external natural things changed, under the very hands of the priest as it were, into the Body and Blood of the beloved Son of God, so that the external rite is merely the *signum*, the sign, of a thing infinitely greater.

In the very midst of Mass, the great rite of the Christian sacrifice, something happens which is like the fire that came down from heaven to consume the sacrifice laboriously prepared by Elias on Mount Carmel. The whispered prayer of the Christian priest: *Ut nobis Corpus et Sanguis fiat dilectissimi Filii tui Domini nostri Jesu Christi, that it may become for us the Body and Blood of Thy most beloved Son, Our Lord Jesus Christ,* is answered.

The sacred words of the Consecration are uttered, and the sacrificial rite, which till then knew only the natural elements of bread and wine, has its meaning expanded to an infinite degree. The Body of Christ and the Blood of Christ have succeeded to bread and wine, and yet the ceremony goes on without hesitation, without any external signs betraying the transformation which has taken place. The sign becomes reality.

All along, when at the Offertory the priest was offering up natural bread and wine, and was speaking to God of this bread and wine, he was thinking higher thoughts, he was dreaming of Flesh and Blood, the Flesh and the Blood of the Son of God. In the very midst of the rite the dream becomes a reality, Christ's Body and Blood are present under the external signs of bread and wine. Melchizedek offered bread and wine in their natural state; his was a true sacrifice expressed in natural gifts, of a finite value. Christ on Calvary offered up His Body and His Blood under no symbol, under no sign, but with an astonishing realism of mortal conditions; this was a sacrifice of infinite worth. The Christian priest has gifts from the field and the vineyard, like Melchizedek; he has also the Body born of the Virgin, the Blood that comes from Mary's veins. But he never has the Body unless he first have the bread, nor the Blood without the wine. This is the *mysterium*, this is the *sacramentum*.

The Christian could never have been so clear and simple in his outlook when he stands at the altar unless he had been taught by the Lord Himself. He does what the Master did. It is a lesson inculcated by Him in a most special way: "Christ, who is a high priest forever after the order of Melchizedek, offered bread and wine."[63] Not only has he learned the lesson, watching the Lord at the Last Supper and doing what He did; the secret of the sacrifice *in mysterio, in sacramento*, lies in this, that at a given moment Infinite Power steps in to make all the signs and symbols into truth, into reality. Christ's consecrating power, exerted for the first time at the Last Supper, remains with the Christian Church, with the official Christian priesthood, to the end of time. This consecrating power is not the same thing as the sacrifice itself; but it is the *conditio sine qua non* which transforms the figurative sacrifice of bread and wine into an infinite oblation.

I said at the beginning that the Christian is full of the thought of the one great sacrifice of Calvary. It is a living faith in him, a burning fire. The daily sacrifice of the Church, far from turning his thoughts away and directing them into other channels, is the same thing made present. It is the same immolation, not merely symbolical, but *in mysterio, in sacramento*. Blood was poured out on Calvary, the Blood of the Son of God. Blood is poured out on the Christian altar, under a sign indeed, but in real truth. To be *in mysterio et in sacramento* is to be as real as to be *in natura*.

In mysterio, in sacramento, there is a true immolation, and the Christian at sacrifice knows that, in his own way, he has seen all that was seen by those who looked on Christ when He was transfixed on the Cross: "They shall look on Him whom they pierced."[64] The *Christianus sacrificans* is essentially one who lives in the faith of the Son of God offered up in sacrifice on the *Ara Crucis*, the altar of the Cross. Through his own special privilege, a privilege not possible outside the sphere of Christ, that of being a *sacrificans in mysterio et sacramento*, it is possible for him to have made present again that same divine immolation—*repraesentari* is the centuries-old Latin theological term for that ceaseless miracle. At the moment of consecration his wish is granted him; the bread and wine he has offered up at the beginning of Mass become the Body and Blood of the Son of God.

Let us then give a succinct portrait of him who thus sacrifices *in mysterio et in sacramento*. He is one who never ceases to remember the death of the Lord. He takes bread and wine as the most fitting symbols of Christ's spotless Flesh and generous Blood. He behaves at first sight as one who is offering up a peace sacrifice in bread and wine, in the manner of Melchizedek. But it is soon apparent that his bread and wine are not meant to remain what they are. The Body of Christ on the Cross, the Blood that was poured out, these are the realities that fill his mind, though the realities before his bodily eyes are bread and wine. Yet even at that early stage, when there is indeed nothing but bread and wine, he utters words that more than hint at realities beyond those elements. To his faith, the Body and Blood become more real than the fruit of the earth, than the juice of the grape. Bread and wine become what he would have them, the only worthy Victim of which he can think, the Body and Blood of the Lamb. The words of Consecration do this for him. His humble peace-offering becomes an immolation: for wherever there is blood there is immolation. It matters little whether this be in the "raw" condition of *natura*, or *in mysterio et sacramento*. The Christian sacrificant is not surprised when the tremendous thing has happened. The sacrifice which he began in bread and wine he finishes in the Body and Blood of the beloved Son of God, but from the very beginning his aim was clear to him. And all this he learned from his Lord and Master, who also had the progressive joy of passing from the human rite into the divinest form of sacrifice:

> And He said to them: With desire I have desired to eat this pasch with you, before I suffer.
>
> For I say to you that from this time I will not eat it, till it be fulfilled in the kingdom of God.
>
> And having taken the chalice, He gave thanks and said: Take and divide it among you.
>
> For I say to you that I will not drink of the fruit of the vine, till the kingdom of God come.
>
> And taking bread, He gave thanks and brake and gave to them, saying: This is My Body, which is given for you. Do this for a commemoration of Me.
>
> In like manner, the chalice also, after He had supped, saying: This is the chalice, the new testament in My Blood, which shall be shed for you.[65]

7

Christian Joy

A well-defined joy belongs to the essence of the Christian character. It might be said that joy is a positive act of which every Christian is capable by the very nature of his faith, as he is capable of prayer, of worship, of repentance. And of this act, in its Christian significance, no one is capable in whom there is not the belief in Christ. We are not expected simply to be good-natured and cheerful people; a vague joyousness is not enough for our vocation. But we have a great joy which is ours at all times, which no one can take away from us, which nothing can diminish, and which is not conditioned by any merely human circumstances. "For, behold, I bring you good tidings of great joy that shall be to all the people," said the angel who spoke to the shepherds in the hour of Christ's birth.[66]

Joy, in the classical Christian sense, is not to be considered directly as the fruit of a holy life, though we do not exclude such kind of joy—that joy which is one of the fruits of the Spirit. Our joyfulness is antecedent to anything we do, to any sanctity we practice; it is an element of Christianity that stands by itself, independently of our conduct, as faith stands by itself. Its justification is not in us but outside ourselves.

To say that only those Christians have a right to be joyful to whom their conscience bears witness they are leading a life of godliness would be a very sad blunder in Christian psychology. There is an independent, an *a priori* joy for all of us, which is not a result but a cause, which does not come from our conduct, but shapes our conduct, which is more operative than passive, which, in a word, belongs institutionally to the very beginnings of the Christian dispensation, as truly as the Christian sacrifice, the Christian sacrament, the Christian prayer.

This institutional Christian joy—I do hope that my reader will not be startled by this combination of terms—is clearly enunciated by Our Lord in Saint John's Gospel: "You have heard that I said to you: I go away, and I come unto you. If you loved Me, you would indeed be glad, because I go to the Father: for the Father is greater than I."[67]

It is the only passage in which Our Lord tells the Apostles to be glad for something that concerns Him directly, not for something that concerns themselves. Very often He bids them be joyful: "Be glad and rejoice, for your reward is very great in heaven."[68] "But yet rejoice not in this, that the spirits are subject unto you: but rejoice in this, that your names are written in heaven."[69] "Hitherto, you have not asked anything in My name. Ask, and you shall receive; that your joy may be full."[70]

In all these glorious promises and declarations the reason given for the joy is that the Christian soul has been enriched or has been favored in some way. The joy comes from a personal advantage; it is essentially a result, the effect of a previous cause. But this renders the words first quoted all the more striking and remarkable for their novelty and singularity. Christ asks for joy, commands joy as the duty of the true lover, over an event that must primarily be a privation for His disciples, the benefit of which is all for Himself personally, directly, nay exclusively: His passage unto the Father. This joy leaves the disciple a mere spectator, though a loving one indeed.

We know the meaning of the profoundly mysterious phrase: "the passage unto the Father." It implies the final and permanent glorification of the Son even in those portions of His being in which, as God Incarnate, Jesus had not as yet been glorified. The Father is essentially eternal, unchanging, unassailable glory and happiness. To pass unto the Father is to enter into complete participation of the supreme triumph of divine life. The Father is greater, not in Person, but in circumstance, because Jesus while here on earth is subject to suffering, to sadness, to ignominy, to death. No such darkness can impinge on the Father who is all Light, in whom there is no manner of darkness. The passage unto the Father is a journey which will end on the summits of divine happiness, from which there will be no return. Christ's departure unto the Father, Christ's Ascension to the Father, Christ's sitting at the right hand of the Father, are all of them wonderful metaphors to state the greatest of all human events: the glorification, final, unlimited, irrevocable, of Jesus Christ in every fiber of His being as God-Man: "For which cause, God also hath exalted Him and hath given Him a name which is above all names: that in the name of Jesus every knee should bow, of those that are in heaven, on earth, and under the earth: and that every tongue should confess that the Lord Jesus Christ is in the glory of God the Father."[71]

Though every tongue sooner or later, willingly or reluctantly, will confess that Jesus is in the glory of God the Father, for the lover of Christ to do so now, wherever he may find himself, is that joy which I call the institutional joy, because its cause is a fact that stands like a divine creation in the very center of the spiritual universe: Christ's supreme and unassailable happiness since the hour of His Resurrection from the dead. The passage unto the Father is, of course, reminiscent of the passage of the children of Israel through the Red Sea to liberty. Christ is our Passover, our Pasch, because of the deep laws of His wonderful personality. He is as one who passed from one state to another, as though the two states had been poles apart, as light and darkness, liberty and captivity.

The great contrast which is implied in the word "passage"— "Jesus knowing that His hour was come, that He should pass out of this world to the Father"[72]—is one of the great mysteries concerning the Person of Christ. We say, in our theology of the Incarnation, that Our Lord, as man, from the very beginning of His existence in His Mother's womb, had in His human soul a clear vision of God, of the Father; He was *comprehensor*, One who was in His intellect already in the highest heavens. He had every kind of glory in the way of knowledge; He was infinitely beyond sin; the heavens stood open before His gaze, and grace went through all His limbs as a boundless stream of the waters of Life. Where then was the captivity, the darkness, the absence from the Father? Not in His intellect, not in His will, not in anything positive; but He was absent from the Father because in some portion of His human nature the glory of the Father was not present, through a mysterious and miraculous providence, so that mankind might be redeemed through suffering. In some powers of His soul Christ could be sad, in His body Christ could feel pain; above all, through an unspeakably merciful retention of life in the higher regions of His personality, death could enter into the lower spheres of His personality. This was the dark Egypt from which His Pasch took Him away. So the glorification of Christ, that supreme evidence of the Father's love for Jesus, means this, that where Jesus was sad before, He is happy now; where He was subject to pain before, He now has divine refreshment; where He could be struck by death He has power to destroy all death. Unless we raise Christ infinitely above such contingencies we do not make that profession which Saint Paul exacts of us, that our tongues should profess that the Lord Jesus is in the glory of the Father.

This then is the Christian attitude; it is in this way that the Christian rejoices. He is a *Christianus gaudens* in virtue of the mystery of Christ's glorification, not directly in virtue of any benefit that makes himself into something holy. This *gaudium Christianum*, Christian joy, is a great act; but it is only doing voluntarily, out of love, what all creation will have to do later: to profess that the Lord Jesus is in the glory of God the Father.

This joy of the Christian is the highest act of spiritual unselfishness. "If you loved Me, you would indeed be glad because I go to the Father." As such it does not come natural to man. It is not to be found anywhere save where Christ is actually recognized as the Lord. It does not exist in vague, chiaroscuro forms of Christianity. Such modes of religion can rejoice only in what they feel. The Christian rejoices in what he sees in the exalted Christ. This *gaudium Christianum* implies knowledge, thought, wisdom in the things of Christ. We are expected to give a reason for His words: "For the Father is greater than I." Mere religious sentiment, a sort of vague affection for Christ, however well meant, will not produce that gladness which Christ wants to see in us as the supreme test of friendship. We must, of course, above all things, become wise in the mysteries of Christ's personality.

There is an unmistakable note of hesitancy in Our Lord's great utterance: "If you loved Me, you would indeed be glad." Did they not love their Master? We know that they loved Him intensely.

But of that objective love, which was more than an affection, which was a clear comprehension of the real issues that mattered, they had so far given no proof.

This is a lesson to us: that true *gaudium Christianum* of which we speak here does not come to us without an effort. Affectionate devotion to Christ is easier than this rejoicing in the supreme glories of the risen Savior. There may even be a danger that affection might find itself more at home with a Christ less removed from the sadness of our daily life. We are liable to create for ourselves a picture of Him which is more in conformity with our longing for His companionship than with our faith in His glorious triumph.

"Danger" is not too strong a word to use. Are we not in constant peril of lowering the Person of Christ to our sentiments, instead of uplifting our feelings as Saint Paul wants us to do? "For let this mind be in you, which was also in Christ Jesus."[73] It is, of course, an irrefragable truth that Jesus Christ is now in the glory of the Father and that no possible suffering could in any sense be predicated of Him there, nor any kind of sadness or sentiment incompatible with the Lord of Glory and the Sovereign Master of heaven and earth. If we speak at all of Christ as being grieved by the sins of men, their infidelities, their ingratitudes, we can only mean those things in the metaphorical sense, imitating Scripture when it speaks of God as being touched inwardly with sorrow of heart at the wickedness of the children of men before the Flood. For Christ to feel sadness now would be tantamount to His being no longer in the glory of the Father or to His having abandoned His risen state.

Sometimes one comes across strange hesitancies in pious souls on this very subject, which reveal a lowering of that sense of joy which comes to us from Christ's passage unto the Father. There is even for some naive spirits a temptation to attribute Christ's presence in the Eucharistic mystery a diminution of that perfect state of glory and impassibility. All such sentiments are, of course, no gain to the Church; they come from an affection that lacks the same light that Christ also sought in His disciples when He said: "If you loved Me, you would indeed be glad, because I go to the Father." If there is one principle that is paramount in the Catholic doctrine of the Eucharist it is this: that the Eucharist on earth cannot be different in the smallest matter from the Christ who is in the glory of the Father, except in the sacramental appearance.

We think, of course, of Christ in His abasement in His mortal days; we also see the sufferings of Christ's mystical Body, and we are keenly conscious of the fact that He is persecuted in His members. Still, we know with Saint Paul that the Christ whose voice comes from heaven and says, "Why persecutest thou Me?" is one whose glory is great beyond words. Paul, years after, when speaking before King Agrippa, had not forgotten the dazzling of his mind as well as of his bodily eyes: "At midday, O king, I saw in the way a light from heaven, above the brightness of the sun, shining round about me and them that were in company with me."[74] It is to such a One we offer our sympathies when we see Him persecuted in His children.

8

The Christian at Work

Work is the crucible of the Christian faith; one might almost be tempted to say that it is its purgatory here on earth. The world teems with work and it would be wrong to say that the activities of mankind are, in their bulk, evil; it is only as an exception that they are bad, normally the enterprises and undertakings of the children of men are fundamentally good. In the midst of these great activities of the human race stands the Christian Church, and unless she were active too, she could not endure for any length of time. In all her other qualities her excellence is easily manifest; her power of prayer, her spiritual superiority are readily accepted; but has she also a real superiority of action, are her works as manifestly divine as is her prayer?

The world does not pray, but it works, and it works well. So we have this phenomenon which I call a crucible and a purgatory, the unceasing contrast between the successes of merely human activities and the successes of those which are essentially Christian.

The contrast, at first sight, at least, is often very painful. We suffer keenly at times from our obvious inferiorities in the field of human productiveness. Is it not the one instance in which Christ seems to allude to His own disciples in a disparaging fashion? "The children of this world are wiser in their generation than the children of light."[75]

It is evident that in this matter of work the lines of demarcation between the children of light and the children of this world are less clearly laid down than in the more spiritual spheres of Christian grace. Many of our good deeds are the boast of men who do not worship Christ; there are services rendered to the race by modern states which, in their material extent and in the efficacy of their application, it is impossible for the Church to emulate.

Moral virtue, as we all know, is so common outside the definitely Christian influence that its existence there is one of the most insidious arguments against the divine claims of the Catholic Church. As for the works of the mind—science in all its branches—it would be futile to pretend that the Church, at any rate today, holds a leading position. Our faith as Christians is constantly being chastened and tried by these visible victories of the prudence of the children of this world; but it is only a trial, it is not a defeat. The gold of true Christian activity has to pass through this crucible of constant comparison with those worldly successes which surround it and almost hide it from view, as a great fire will envelop the very metal which it is to cleanse, and will render it, for the moment, invisible.

The work of the Gospel—to give it its classical name—is the highest of all human activities; there is more genius in it, there is more prudence in it, there is more dexterity in it, than in any other undertaking of man. The Christian work is as supernatural and as divine in its character and its origin as is the Christian prayer, as is the Christian sacrifice. It is an activity which differs profoundly from all other exertions of men in the pursuit of their aims; but the one need which is urgent is this, that we should have eyes that are able to discriminate between the tools of the Spirit and the tools of nature, for nothing is easier in practice than to make this confusion in the choice of the instruments we are using. Nature has a marvelous resourcefulness, and many a worker with the best intentions uses nature's tools when he ought to be handling the instruments of the Spirit.

What do we mean here by work? We do not directly allude to that vast realm of spiritual realities which all Scripture and theology agree in calling "good works"; they are the fruits of the tree of life, they are the necessary concomitant of faith—for faith without good works would be dead—the whole Christian life with all its sanctities is work; it is the merit that accumulates and that will be crowned with eternal reward. Nor by work do we in this chapter mean supernatural merit. We mean, truly, something more external, that is in the nature of an enterprise, of a conquest.

Christian work is in its more restricted sense essentially the effort of the Church and of her children to establish the Gospel: "Be thou vigilant: labor in all things: do the work of an evangelist: fulfill thy ministry."[76] We might write endlessly on Christian work considered as the fertility of our faith. It is the perennial insistence of the Church of Christ that unless we bear fruit in Christ our faith alone will not save us. All Christians, of course, are operative in that sense, and most of them labor with unremitting energy. This class of work is aptly described in Christ's own language as the fruit of the tree of justice: "You have not chosen Me: but I have chosen you; and have appointed you, that you should go and bring forth fruit; and that your fruit should remain."[77] The faithful man who is thus bearing fruit of justice is not the *Christianus operans* in the technical sense of this chapter, he is instead the fruit-bearing branch on that Vine which is Christ; he would be the *Christianus frugifer*, the fruit bearer, and thus we may describe him elsewhere. The work of the evangelist, *opus evangelistae*, as Saint Paul so aptly calls it, is, of course, meritorious in its turn, but it has a kind of independence of personal merit on which Saint Paul more than once insists: "For if I preach the gospel, it is no glory to me: for a necessity lieth upon me. For woe is unto me if I preach not the gospel. For if I do this thing willingly, I have a reward: but if against my will, a dispensation is committed unto me."[78] Again he admits the possibility of doing this work and yet not reaching eternal salvation: "I chastise my body and bring it into subjection: lest perhaps, when I have preached to others, I myself should become a castaway."[79]

It is evident from an even superficial study of the apostolic writings that in this matter of external activities practical difficulties arose very early among the faithful. The great illumination which was their spiritual privilege rendered them either contemptuous of the necessities of ordinary human life or excessively hopeful concerning the new dispensation; they thought themselves exempt from the solicitudes of daily life: "We entreat you, brethren, that you abound more: and that you use your endeavor to be quiet; and that you do your own business and work with your hands, as we commanded you: and that you walk honestly towards them that are without: and that you want nothing of any man's."[80]

It is really part of that Christian fertility of which we have spoken that we should fulfill all the duties of human life just as other men; the difference is in the spirit: Christian charity ought to permeate our daily occupations and make of them an unceasing service of Christ in His members. It cannot be denied that his lesson of human usefulness was in need of reiteration even in apostolic days: "If any man have not care of his own and especially of those of his house, he hath denied the faith and is worse than an infidel."[81] With an insistence which we might almost call modern, the great Apostle wants his Christians to take a share in all the work of the human family: "It is a faithful saying, and these things I will have thee affirm constantly, that they who believe in God may be careful to excel in good works. These things are good and profitable unto men.... And let our men also learn to excel in good works for necessary uses: that they be not unfruitful."[82]

But this, again, does not constitute the *Christianus operans*, specifically so-called.

As through a wonderful disposition of divine providence the mystery of Christ is to be made known to men through their fellows, a new kind of work has been created through the Gospel—the manifestation of Christ unto all creatures.

This is that specifically Christian work which I have been trying to distinguish from the other activities of man, considered in the natural and in the supernatural state. This is the *opus Christi*, the *opus Domini*, the *opus evangelistae* of Saint Paul: "Because for the work of Christ he came to the point of death."[83] "If Timothy come, see that he be with you without fear: for he worketh the work of the Lord, as I also do."[84]

A moment's reflection will be enough to make it clear what a task God entrusted to man when He made him the ambassador of Christ for all time; the very nature and size of the commission implies a fitness in the workman which must be entirely *sui generis*, for which there is no parallel in the history of the world. We all admit *a priori* that a wholly new spiritual equipment is necessary for the supreme purpose of converting the world unto Christ, but in practice it will not always be easy to distinguish between the ordinary and the extraordinary, between the natural and the supernatural, in the means for an end so wholly beyond man's capacity. The gifts which Christ has bestowed upon His

Church for the carrying out of her great mission are essentially activities that proceed from man, so that they are constantly intertwined with man's ordinary and natural powers.

For instance—anticipating here what we shall say presently— the Son of God has left in His Church the totally supernatural gift of teaching, not only in a general way, but with the specific quality of the Gospel: that is to say the Church has an entirely new grace, that of expounding the Gospel.

Now it is evident that such a gift could not be operative unless many other powers of man came into play. The teacher of the Gospel will be one who has a sufficiently high standard of education; most likely he will speak a language whose perfection he has learned in the schools; he may be endowed with all the qualities of an orator. At first sight it will seem that he is only a man speaking like other men, though he preach doctrines which are not of man, but of God, and it will not be apparent that his exposition of such doctrines is more than the effort of a human mind. Now this would be a supreme mistake. Through all that natural talent there runs a supernatural flame, that special gift which Christ has given to His Church, the power of teaching. For this is complete Catholicism, to believe not only in the divine origin of Christian truth and in the supernatural grace that touches man's heart and mind, opening them to the divine truth, but also in those special gifts which are the external instruments of the Church in her great work of preaching heavenly doctrine to all creatures.

The term *gratiae gratis datae* (graces gratuitously given[85]) stands for a vast world of supernatural realities, a world which can easily become obscured to our eyes, not because it is distant, but because there is between it and our consciousness another reality, that of natural human activity. When we see the brilliant institutions of the Church for the propagation and maintenance of

Catholic thought we might easily be misled, and see in such manifestations a cause when they are only a result. The impression might be created that on the whole the Church works with the same methods as do all other institutions which are keen on conquering the human mind. But the real facts are far different. The Church's powers are essentially those *gratiae gratis datae* concerning which we have authentic descriptions in the apostolic writings. The history of the mighty Christian work is this: the Apostles were sent forth by Christ, practically without any of the equipment of human talents, yet more powerful men never set out on a mission; they were men prepared for their calling with the supreme skill of divine workmanship; Christ the Son of God had given them all power. Now this was a permanent institution, not a transient dispensation; in other words, the supernatural gifts of the Apostles were bestowed on them, not because they were by nature so helpless, but because the work they were sent out to do could not be achieved, either in their time or in any other by different methods. So when later on—and this happened very soon—much human talent was found in the Church, the apostolic gifts did not take a secondary place, much less were they superseded; for that would have meant a radical change in the supernatural order instituted by Christ. The natural gifts of the early doctors, as of the doctors of later periods, could only be in an ancillary position with regard to the permanent and everlasting powers of the grace of the Christian apostolate.

The classical exponent of those essentially Christian powers which do the work of the Gospel is, as we all know, Saint Paul. The word *gratia* is used by the Apostle indiscriminately for the interior, supernatural transformation of man's soul and for those exterior activities which are the *conditio sine qua non* of the success of the Gospel in this world. It is not always easy at first sight to see whether, in a given passage of the Acts of the Apostles or the

Epistles, the word "grace" stands for the internal gift of sanctification or the external, heavenly-given power of doing the work of Christ; in fact, to the mind of the early Church all activity in connection with the propagation of the Name of Christ was looked upon in the light of the Holy Spirit, and was considered as an outpouring of the Spirit. Saint Paul contrasts the former impotence of his neophytes with their present power and energy, but their newly found talents are entirely supernatural in their origin:

> You know that when you were heathens, you went to dumb idols, according as you were led. Wherefore, I give you to understand that no man, speaking by the Spirit of God, saith Anathema to Jesus. And no man can say The Lord Jesus, but by the Holy Spirit. Now there are diversities of graces, but the same Spirit. And there are diversities of ministries, but the same Lord. And there are diversities of operations, but the same God, who worketh all in all. And the manifestation of the Spirit is given to every man unto profit.[86]

There follows the famous enumeration of the gifts, and the Apostle's declaration as to their relative value in the spiritual order; finally, "And God indeed hath set some in the church: first apostles, secondly prophets, thirdly doctors: after that miracles: then the graces of healings, helps, governments, kinds of tongues, interpretations of speeches."[87] Again, in the Epistle to the Ephesians Saint Paul describes the scope of all that supernatural organization of work in the following terms: "The perfecting of the saints, the work of the ministry, the edifying of the body of Christ."[88]

Much has been written by men versed in the interpretation of the Scriptures concerning the exact meaning of all those gifts described by Saint Paul; it is not our purpose here to make a special study of the various gifts, but one thing is certain and beyond all cavil, the early Church depended completely for its success and external maintenance on the exercise of specific gifts which were of an executive nature. The *Christianus operans* of the Apostolic days was a clearly defined personality, he had talents which no other men possessed, he was not a religious philosopher, he was a power.

The question in which we all are interested is this: have we anything in common with the first Christian age in this matter of spiritual powers? Of course none of us have any doubts as to our community of spirit with those times; we share in the same grace—if we consider grace as the life-giving quality of the soul— we share in the faith, in the hope, in the charity of the faithful of all ages. But has there not been a distinct change in the methods of doing the work of the Gospel? The answer, of course, must be in the negative. It is against all the principles of Christian continuity of life that any heavenly gifts should at a given time become obsolete and superfluous, should be superseded by energies of a lower order; nothing could sound more untheological, for instance, than to say that miracles are not granted to the Church today because she is now more rich in human resources than she was in other ages; this would be tantamount to saying that a human dispensation had taken the place of one that was divine. The *gratiae gratis datae* are as much with us today as they were with the early Church; we have miracles, we have prophecies, we have the gift of tongues, we have ministries, we have the whole galaxy of the gifts of the Spirit with us, we need but look round about us to see them everywhere. Nothing is more evident than the fact that the Catholic Church of today is full of marvelous powers which can only be described in such terms as were used by Saint Paul himself when he spoke of the diversities of graces in his own times.

It is necessary, however, in order to see the presence of these *gratiae gratis datae*, to classify carefully such phenomena of the spiritual life as are exhibited by the Church today. If we have become less attentive to the existence of those special gifts of the Spirit in our midst it is chiefly because we have given wrong names to supernatural manifestations, we have confused one set of gifts with another. There is in the Catholic Church today a wonderful amount of sanctity and charity, but there is also a most varied activity which is not the same thing as sanctity, though it be most edifying and most imposing as a supernatural manifestation. Wherever we go we find excellent work done; the teaching orders are eminent in their profession; the preaching of Christian truth and morality is unwavering and uncompromising in a world that dares no longer hold any convictions with positive certainty; the external administration of the Church shows no sign of weakness; from the Pope down to the youngest priest there is the undiminished belief that the Church's government is entirely divine in its authority and root principles. The worship of the Church is not only artistic, it is profoundly real, devoid of all superstition and hypocrisy. There is in the Church an immense grace of mercy, a facility to succor human suffering which is totally different from the pseudo-philanthropy of modern states.

All these things and many more, what are they but gifts of the Spirit, graces which are not directly for the sanctification of the individual, but for the building up of the Body of Christ in charity? It is true that all such activities are constantly intermixed with human nature, with human talent, but that is no reason why we should fail to distinguish the innate and incommunicable traits of the supernatural which are an integral part of their character. In no gift is this blending of the two talents, the supernatural and the natural, more baffling than in that gift of speech—of all the diversities of graces the most permanent and the most universal—the power to expound the faith of Christ to every class of mind, from the child to the highly-cultured modern man. That such a power exists in the Catholic Church today, and this to a wonderful degree, is evident to all, but we might make the mistake of thinking that our competence and our facility are merely the result of natural education. Such is not the case. Our priests and our teachers have received a gift, and it is in virtue of that gift that they illumine and convince souls. Education is most welcome, but it does not constitute the Christian preacher; he is what he is through a gift of persuasion that was already possessed by those who carried the Gospel message to the heathen of the first century.

Saint Thomas Aquinas, in his great work on Christian ethics, takes it for granted without a moment's hesitation that the *gratiae gratis datae* of the early Church are as much part of later Christianity as are faith and hope and charity. That great classifier of spiritual phenomena places under the heading of *gratiae gratis datae* all those marvels of which present-day hagiography is as full as any previous accounts of the lives of God's servants. Ecstasies, rapts,[89] visions, knowledge of unseen things, transports of the spirit, heavenly voices, marvelous abstractions of the mind, and all such phenomena, according to Saint Thomas, are manifestations of the Spirit for the profit of the Church, not necessarily for the sanctification of the individual recipient of them. Now are we not today surrounded by such outpourings of the supernatural? Have we not our miracles, now here, now there, as in previous ages? In fact, the strengthening and the extending of the Kingdom of Christ is carried out today, as it always was carried out, through a multitude of mysterious factors which have one thing in common, that they are not of earthly origin, though they may be contained in the earthen vessels of human life.

There is in these gifts a certain element of uncertainty and elusiveness for which Saint Paul makes due allowance: "Extinguish not the Spirit. Despise not prophecies. But prove all things:

hold fast that which is good."[90] So likewise in his great enumeration of the gifts in the First Epistle to the Corinthians, the Apostle insinuates that mistakes may be made, not only as to the relative value of those gifts, but even as to their reliability in individual instances:

> If therefore the whole church come together into one place, and all speak with tongues, and there come in unlearned persons or infidels, will they not say that you are mad?[91]

There is a certain critical sense which is desirable in this matter and which is not the same thing as contempt of the Spirit:

> The spirits of the prophets are subject to the prophets. For God is not the God of dissension, but of peace: as also I teach in all the churches.[92]

There is an important lesson to be learned from this attitude of Saint Paul towards the spiritual powers. Those endowments have not that certainty which is the proper quality of faith, many human elements may be mingled with them; this is allowed for: their efficiency does not depend upon their being unmistakably apprehended at all times as being of divine origin, faith alone can lay claim to such a clearness of position; it is not necessary to have metaphysical certainty concerning an individual miracle in order to be edified by it. Once more, such a degree of certainty is the exclusive quality of the Catholic creed; the operative gifts are much more human.

So there is all over the Catholic Church an unceasing and most varied manifestation of supernatural power which has a great influence in building up the Body of Christ, but it would be vain to expect that each individual manifestation could be analyzed and proved to be exclusively supernatural. The Spirit works with infinite generosity and it is sufficient for Him that the souls redeemed by Christ be edified in charity. There may be reasons why at times certain of the manifestations of the Spirit be subjected to a close scrutiny and be analyzed by human science, as is the case for instance with some of the Lourdes miracles which do not pass muster unless the Bureau des Constatations[93] has pronounced on them; for wise reasons such human precautions are resorted to at times by ecclesiastical authority. But it would be a grave mistake and a grievous loss to Catholic life were we to maintain that the gifts of the Spirit would be no evidence that God is amongst us unless human science were satisfied as to their authenticity. The Spirit is free to act as He lists: "The Spirit breatheth where He will and thou hearest His voice: but thou knowest not whence He cometh and whither He goeth."[94]

The *charismata* of the Catholic Church are life. They are deeply interwoven with all the conditions of human existence; they may be easily counterfeited, precisely because they are stirrings of the unconscious regions of the human soul; it is more directly their mission to strengthen than to illuminate. All over the world the Christian people know that they are constantly being helped and succored, comforted and consoled, by the powers of the Christian ministry, by the words of the Christian mystic, by the exhortations of the Christian preacher, by the prayers of the friends of God, by the marvelous phenomena of Catholic sanctity; they are certain of these things and wisdom is justified by her own children.

9

The Christian in Temptation

We are much in need of a complete theological treatise on temptation. It would save us from many a shallow judgment of human events if we were simple enough, or instructed enough, to admit the fact that temptation is an integral part of the scheme of things as willed and ordained by the Creator. Whenever there occurs one of the catastrophic events that change the conditions under which human souls work out their salvation, every possible and imaginable reason is given in order to account for the incidence of the cataclysm at a given time, or in a given part of the world. The self-appointed philosophers of history all have their pet theories concerning the mental soundness of the human race. The neglect and forgetfulness by mankind of their favorite spiritual remedy brought about, according to them, the disastrous event. Thus some will say that we owe the Reformation in England and all its evils to a bad system of the ownership of land, in which the Church was the principal culprit.

Few thinkers, except the very greatest, have the courage to say that a special temptation may have come over men which had not come before. As for the landownership trouble, it existed at many other periods and in many other places, without a "Reformation" coming out of it. Human history contains the element of temptation as much as it contains the element of human freedom, and temptation belongs to the spiritual growth of mankind as ice and snow belong to the preservation of life in nature. So there is as truly an orthodox theology on temptation as there is an unorthodox one, and the Christian must find himself in temptation, as he finds himself in other preordained situations, for his ultimate salvation. The Christian, at given stages of his life, is one who is tempted, one who is directly under the providence of temptation. His temptation, either individual or corporate, is no haphazard thing, is not a lower level into which he has sunk. It is a direct call to the Mountain of Christ, the Mount of Temptation.

The manner in which the Evangelist introduces the story of Christ's temptation is truly astonishing: "Then Jesus was led by the Spirit into the desert, to be tempted by the devil."[95] Christ's journey into the desert, from the banks of the Jordan where the heavens had been opened above Him, is described as a precipitate flight from the scene of glory to the dark country of temptation. "And immediately the Spirit drove Him out into the desert."[96] "And Jesus being full of the Holy Spirit, returned from the Jordan and was led by the Spirit into the desert."[97]

There is such an evident purpose and scheme in all this that one cannot help picturing to oneself Our Lord going forward to the temptation with as firm a step as He had gone to the glory of His baptism at the hands of John, with the splendid witness of the Father and the Holy Spirit. Those forty days of temptation were not a period of dereliction, they were days full of sanctity. It is not, of course, possible for us to understand the nature of that titanic struggle between Christ and Satan in the wilderness; it is not called a "struggle" in the Scriptures; the word employed is "temptation."

A struggle is a clear issue; a temptation of necessity contains an element of doubt and obscurity. In temptation there are distinct allurements and attractions to an opposite course; not so in a struggle where the minds of the combatants are made up. The words of the tempter to Christ have plausibility. It is certain that when Christ left the Jordan for the desert, He walked from light into darkness. Something sinister surrounded Him on all sides. It was the very antithesis of the splendors that had cast a ray of glory on the waters of the Jordan. But more than anything else the resoluteness with which Christ placed Himself under the dark cloud is most strongly shown.

It is difficult for our weak spiritual constitutions to find satisfaction in the thought that the anguish of a temptation is as much part and parcel of our Christian life as the exaltation of our prayer. We may take it for granted that the Christian, like Christ Himself, is being placed in temptation, as he is being put into other spiritual states, by the act of God. If such a prospect were to frighten us, a glance at Christ, hastily making His way into the barren country beyond the Jordan, ought to bring us the assurance that temptation in itself cannot be an evil thing. Christ went to His temptation as later He went to His Cross. In such a matter one must perforce speak in the abstract, as it were, taking the phenomenon of temptation ideally. There is this difference between Christ's passion and His temptation in the desert, that the former cannot be isolated and distinguished from the human wickedness which planned and brought about His death on the Cross. No human agency drove Jesus into the desert to be tempted by Satan, but the Spirit Himself, in this divine instance we see temptation in its simplicity as an ordinance of the Father.

Though such clarity of outline be rarely perceptible in ordinary temptation, one mysterious fact underlies all the perplexities of our human difficulties, that temptation for its own sake is much more frequent in our lives than we imagine. The Christian is one who must pass through temptation: it is the very badge of his tribe.

The Catholic theology of temptation furnishes us with the truest reading of Church history; the holy men and women of all times are found in the state of temptation, by the will of God. Popes, bishops, leaders of the army of Christ, are taken into the desert of temptation. Religious orders are given by God their temptations as truly as they are partakers in the other riches of Christ. The Catholic Church in her corporate existence as the mystical Body of Christ is taken into barren places and through dark periods to be tempted by the devil.

It is indeed a positive relief to one's mind to be able to have this faith in the divinely appointed mission of temptation. It sets one free from the incubus of a false historical presentment of the long life of the Catholic Church. The countless difficulties that have beset her course are not of necessity the result of her short-comings; a most perfect Church may be carried hither and thither by evil agencies, as the spotless body of Christ was taken through the air, His soul, of course, remaining untouched by the hands of the tempter. No true reading of Christianity is possible except in the light of the theology of temptation. But once that light is thrown on the apparently checkered career of Catholicism, as a beam from a lighthouse, what a difference of meaning and outline appears!

Catholic historians themselves have not always remembered that the Church whose long life they have undertaken to chronicle is the Bride of Christ, who follows the Bridegroom into the barren hills beyond Jordan as faithfully as up to the summit of

Mount Tabor. In my daily life I prefer to look on my afflicted fellow-Christian as one who is chastised by God Himself. The natural, unchristian mind, of course, of which there is so much in each one of us, will prompt us to other conclusions. Men's troubles, we say, are of their own making, and they get what they deserve. Such words seem to come from a thirst for justice, but in reality they express a quite pagan attitude. Most unsupportable are those men who never have anything but words of reprobation when anywhere in the Church of Christ there is trouble. I am, of course, alluding to Catholic critics of current events. They are wonderfully cocksure concerning the origin of the persecution in Mexico, the difficulties in Spain, and the backwardness of Catholic causes generally. If only people had done what they ought to have done, say they, there would have been nothing to disturb the serene prosperity of Catholicism. As often as not the critic has a nostrum of his own which, if applied, would have been the healing of the nations.

It never seems to enter the heads of these good men that agencies of an entirely different order may be at work. "Neither hath this man sinned, nor his parents; but that the works of God should be made manifest in him."[98] Such was Christ's reply to the Twelve when, being the good Jews they were, seeing a man who was blind from his birth they had asked, "Rabbi, who hath sinned, this man or his parents, that he should be born blind?"

In these days when the prevailing humanism of the world at large is not without its subtle effects even on theologians, objections will be brought forward against the notion that the children of God are being placed in temptation, which would not have been entertained by our forefathers, stronger in the faith. It is, of course, the "Good Father" theology which has no room for the classical doctrine of the *Christianus tentatus*. God is a good Father, it is said, how could He find it in His heart to leave His children in the perplexities of temptation? The greatest misfortune that has befallen modern religious thought is the setting aside of all the other divine names for the one name of Father, as if this one alone expressed God adequately. One of the oldest Christian classics, an anonymous one to boot, is the Greek treatise *On the Divine Names*. If popularized today it would supply something greatly needed. No single human word fully expresses the functions of the Deity; and even when all human terms that are available have been pressed into service to describe God's relationship with man, there always remains this glorious certainty that God deals with men in a way that is entirely His own, that has no name, that is wonderful beyond comprehension.

It is, then, the merit of true Christian theology that it is not scandalized, but edified, by the temptation which God sends to His rational creatures. We may say that a Deity that can afford to leave the created rational being in temptation gives proof of its legitimacy. To draw a parallel: an ancient, well-established dynasty, whose place is in the very heart of a race, can suffer innumerable eclipses and defeats without any one being the less loyal during the period of trial. The usurper, on the contrary, is obliged to be victorious, successful, in everything he undertakes. In continuous, brilliant, manifest success is his only real claim to power. One defeat in the field, one bad year of administration, will put an end to all his prestige. A demiurge could not trust to a providence of temptation; an infinite Creator can afford it on any scale because, in the words of Saint Paul, "God is faithful, who will not suffer you to be tempted above that which you are able: but will make also with temptation issue, that you may be able to bear it."[99]

God has a providence of temptation, as He has a providence of prosperity, and He uses each in turn with equal skill. Is it not this older and vaster comprehension of God's nature that gives to the scriptural presentment of Him a splendor, a power, an interest, that is completely absent from so much of our manmade hymnology? "Although He should kill me, I will trust in Him. But yet I will reprove my ways in His sight. And He shall be my savior: for no hypocrite shall come before His presence."[100] Thus spoke Job, the inspired poet of temptation and its everlasting pattern. Our Scriptures are our only authentic history of God and His ways. They present us with a Power that is so sure of itself that it can let man down to the lowest depth without peril.

To the man who thrice implored the Lord that temptation should be removed from him was given the answer: "My grace is sufficient for thee."[101] God's grace is like the exhilaration of a born warrior in the face of peril. "The Lord is as a man of war, Almighty is His name."[102] It implies no contradiction that God should teach us to pray thus: "Lead us not into temptation," whilst on the other hand He sends us temptation. One point has not been made known to us, namely, why there should be temptation. In temptation God is the *vir pugnator*, the fighting One. In temptation God may be said to meet peril and to take us along with Him. It is in keeping with all we know of God that He should wish us to pray for alleviation in those very things with which He burdens us. We ask God to deliver us from His own wrath: *Ab ira tua, libera nos, Domine*; and there is a special collect in the Roman Missal *pro tentatis et tribulatis*.

We Catholics can be very hard sometimes on our fellow-Catholics when they are unsuccessful. We loudly condemn, when perhaps there is a wonderful providence behind the apparent failure. This comes from our obstinacy in taking merely human views of events. There ought to be in us a continual dread lest we strike those whom the Lord has afflicted. God's anger at this human presumption and rudeness is very great. "And I am angry with a great anger with the wealthy nations: for I was angry a little, but they helped forward the evil."[103] God had been displeased over Jerusalem; Zion received from His hands what she deserved. But the Lord kept a divine measure. The nations, on the contrary, that fell upon her, knew no limits to their ferocity in their slaughter of Israel.

When there are trials and difficulties, heartburnings and failures in the household of the faith, our step in passing the scene of affliction ought to be as light and as careful as it is when we go by the door of a fever-stricken friend. The greatest praise Our Lord bestowed on the Apostles was over this very matter. They looked at Him with awe when they did not grasp the nature of His sorrows: "And you are they who have continued with Me in My temptations."[104]

10

Christian Vigilance

Alertness is a quality easily detected in both man and beast. We all are familiar with the most common type of animal alertness in the watchdog; its quickness to perceive the unusual is an inexhaustible source of interest to the observer. But certain men, too, have a great gift of watchfulness which makes them admirable protectors of their fellowmen. They quickly scent danger in the present or future situation. Now these striking provisions of nature for the security of man have their counterpart in the supernatural gift of vigilance, which is a distinctly permanent and universal feature in every Christian. It is true, of course, that Christian watchfulness is usually spoken of by way of precept. Christians are commanded by Christ Himself to watch, as they are also ordered to pray. But in this manner, as in all other realities of the spiritual life, the command supposes the gift, and the precept has as its prerequisite a special grace. We are told by the Son of God to make constant use of the gift of prudent awareness which His Spirit has put into all of us; otherwise the command would be impossible of fulfillment. So we may consider Christian vigilance as a quality of the baptized man, as a talent, as an instinct possessed by him for the scenting out of danger and recognizing the approach of evil. We may then speak of the *Christianus vigilans*, the watchful Christian, indiscriminately from the point of view of precept and from the point of view of endowment: to be watchful is for him the fulfillment of a duty as well as the exercise of a marvelous power of perception. The comparison with the watchdog is no levity, for the Holy Spirit has not hesitated to make use of it in the Scriptures, though in a disparaging sense. The Prophet Isaiah uses sarcastic words concerning the unworthy ministers of religion: "His watchmen are all blind. They are all ignorant: dumb dogs not able to bark, seeing vain things, sleeping, and loving dreams."[105]

There is, then, in the faithful Christian soul a temperament which seems to be the result of all the other refinements of spirit: the soul is sensitive and fearful, easily alarmed and stirred up. This is more than prudence, as it moves so quickly and acts more by intuition than by a slow procedure of thought. The Christian is the very opposite of that character so vividly described in the passage of Isaiah just quoted. It must be admitted that God has put into the Christian a very special sensitiveness which is his first weapon against the innumerable dangers that beset his salvation. Danger is perceived, not by prudence, but by instinct. Prudence alone would be too slow. In this the Christian differs radically from the heathen, taking the term "heathen" in the same sense as Christ when He says, "And when you are praying, speak not much, as the heathens."[106] Heathenism in this sense means a mind completely devoid of the sense of fear with regard to spiritual evil. It has no alarms, it has no terrors; it is stupidly ignorant of the presence of hostile forces. Now the Christian is the very opposite.

To the heathen he may appear a timid man, filled with un-founded terrors; but in very truth he is no coward, he is a wide-awake warrior, who knows the strength of his enemy. Above all he is endowed with an extraordinary promptness in discovering the wiles of the adversary.

It is indeed a phenomenon easily observed in our own days that "heathenism," that negative attitude towards Christianity which is so widespread in Europe, has as its result a callousness of attitude towards the terrors of the unseen world which to a Catholic is quite incomprehensible. This complete lack of response in so many men could not be called fortitude of spirit, even by the wildest stretch of imagination. It is obviously nothing else than insensibility of mind and heart, a contempt of danger that comes from a complete lack of perception. Such people do not watch, as they do not pray, because there is no kind of recep-tivity in them. They feel neither anxiety nor need, through a sheer negation of life. Perilous doctrines that will inevitably cause the ruination of whole civilizations bring no alarm to them; as often as not they side with the destroying powers. They see in death no sort of solemnity or terror. We often say that this indifference comes from a lack of imagination; but this is a flimsy attenuation of a tragic phenomenon. The real cause of their sad condition is an entire destitution of spiritual and supernatural alertness.

What then is the behavior of the true *Christianus vigilans*? What are the noises, the sounds, the rumors, that alarm him and put him on his guard? For Christian watchfulness is something more than merely care taken not to fall, not to spoil the garment of the soul. The Christian vigilance described for us by Our Lord is evidently to combat the agencies of evil that are as much outside us as within, the "thieves" of His constant warnings. The very house in which we dwell as Christians, the Church of Christ, may be broken into by enemies who will make it their first task not to be discovered, not to be identified. So Christian caution has a much wider scope than mere carefulness over one's own activities. It has to do with a whole world of inimical spirits, both personal and impersonal; it is concerned with thoughts and ideas as directly as with deeds and behavior. There is no greater duty incumbent on the shepherds of the Church than the sifting of doctrines lest false teaching creep in. Saint Paul's recommendations to the elders of Ephesus are the classical scriptural enforcement of the duty of watchfulness in doctrine.

> Take heed to yourselves and to the whole flock, wherein the Holy Spirit hath placed you bishops, to rule the Church of God which He hath purchased with His own blood. I know that after my departure ravening wolves will enter in among you, not sparing the flock. And of your own selves shall arise men speaking perverse things, to draw away disciples after them. Therefore watch, keeping in memory that for three years I ceased not with tears to admonish every one of you, night and day.[107]

In this matter of vigilance the clear-mindedness of the Catholic Church comes into dire conflict with all attitudes that are not completely Christian. It would appear that this gift of alertness is so much the peculiar quality of the one true Church that it is quite incommunicable. It exists nowhere else; a feeble acquiescence in error and doubt is the universal condition of the non-Catholic religious bodies. "Holy Inquisition" may be an odious word in the ears of many, but it is only a Church absolutely sure of herself that dares to inquire into every trend of thought, and, if needful, to proceed further and denounce them as evil and dangerous. One could almost venture the remark that without such spiritual alertness the Church would he quite a different institution, and in order to describe it we should need entirely different words and figures of speech from those we now constantly employ.

We are, then, fully justified in speaking of the *Christianus vigilans*, the watchful Christian. This term classifies him in a very clear and definite manner; it gives his character a sharpness of outline which the other gifts cannot produce. It makes him into a mature, experienced, alert man in the spiritual order. It is the ripeness of years in his supernatural development.

Until we all meet into the unity of faith and of the knowledge of the Son of God, unto a perfect man, unto the measure of the age of the fullness of Christ. That henceforth we be no more children, tossed to and fro and carried about with every wind of doctrine, by the wickedness of men, by cunning craftiness by which they lie in wait to deceive.[108]

11

The Christian and the Eucharist

It is an evident fact in the spiritual order that the mystery of the Eucharist profoundly affects the character of the true Christian. But who can tell to what extent Christian mentality is steeped in the profundities of the Eucharist? One would crave leave to coin a word, so as to be able to call Christians eucharistic beings; for such they are in very truth. In one of the international Eucharistic Congresses held in recent years in Anglo-Saxon lands, the enterprising reporters of the public press gave to the participants in the Congress, who had come from all parts of the globe, the short name of "Eucharists." One could almost plead for the retention of such a designation for our Catholic people. The Christian has not only faith in the mystery of the Eucharist; he has a temperament, a character that makes him a member of that infinitely vast mystery, the sacramental state of the Son of God. How very different from the Christianity that we know would be a Christianity that was not eucharistic! Though a good deal on this aspect of the Christian character is already contained in the *Christianus sacrificans*, the Christian at sacrifice, the riches of the Eucharist are not exhausted by the notion of sacrifice. The Eucharist is the origin of a whole new life for the Christian, subjectively and objectively, in the sense that he is transformed in his own soul by that mystery, and that the exterior world takes on a fresh hue for him through the presence of Christ in the adorable Sacrament.

Saint Paul has not neglected this aspect of the Christian character. The Eucharistic mystery, as sacrifice and as food, is a great reality that brings about the psychological cleavage between the faithful and the infidel:

> I speak as to wise men: judge ye yourselves what I say. The chalice of benediction which we bless, is it not the communion of the Blood of Christ? And the bread which we break, is it not the partaking of the Body of the Lord? For we, being many, are one bread, one body: all that partake of one bread. Behold Israel according to the flesh. Are not they that eat of the sacrifices partakers of the altar? What then? Do I say that what is offered in sacrifice to idols is anything? Or that the idol is anything? But the things which the heathens sacrifice, they sacrifice to devils and not to God. And I would not that you should be made partakers with devils. You cannot drink the chalice of the Lord and the chalice of devils: you cannot be partakers of the table of the Lord and of the table of devils. Do we provoke the Lord to jealousy? Are we stronger than He?[109]

I have quoted this passage in full because it is truly an inexhaustible mine of instruction to us, making us grasp more clearly the nature of our vocation in Christ. As is well known it was a difficulty of daily occurrence with the new converts in the great cities of the heathen world to "fly from the service of idols," for the worship of the false gods permeated everything. We need only listen to historians and archaeologists, or visit the ruins of those cities of an ancient civilization, to realize how omnipresent the idol was. Temples everywhere, and what temples! The smoke of the idolatrous incense in every man's nostrils, the meat of the huge sacrifices sold in every butcher's shop. It was as difficult a task for the early Christian to flee from the service of the idols as it is for us to keep immune from the influence of the public press. There was also in the man or woman newly converted from paganism the atavism that made a complete riddance of inherited complexes no easy matter. Through his faith, in his intellect, he knew, of course, that "an idol is nothing in the world and that there is no God but one."[110]

But as there were "Gods many and Lords many," according to the persuasion of the innumerable pagans who surrounded the Christian convert, the prevailing atmosphere must have been supremely trying and depressing, with triumphant paganism so blatantly sure of itself. After all, by birth and a thousand affiliations he was a member of that society; the crowd psychology held him just as it holds us in the modern world. Then there were the practical difficulties of the daily life; at common repasts, at social banquets, there were the libations to the gods; the meat sold in the shops was meat from the temples, remnants of the lavish animal sacrifices to the deities; and only the strong-minded could detach themselves completely from the impressions created by such an association of ideas.

Now into this heavy atmosphere of oppressive paganism the Christian, in the picture which Saint Paul draws of him, steps like a being from another world in the strength of the Eucharistic mystery. He is a strong athlete through a mystery of Flesh and Blood. He has a secret which gives him from the very start a genuine superiority: "I speak as to wise men." Christians have their own language, their own standards, their own code of values: "Judge ye yourselves what I say." The Apostle puts the issue in an interrogative form to emphasize its certainty and its validity with all Christians: "The chalice of benediction which we bless, is it not the communion of the Blood of Christ? And the bread which we break, is it not the partaking of the Body of the Lord?" Here indeed we have the food and drink of heroes! If such beverage and such meat does not make us different from other men, nothing will. But this resistance to environment thus communicated to the Christian character is not just the self-defense of each individual. It is a great social bond, and fortitude comes from our being infeoffed[111] into a greater life. The mass psychology of paganism is opposed by the power of the Communion of Saints: "For we, being many, are one bread, one body: all that partake of one bread." There is a precedent for this new and supernatural nationalism in the Flesh and Blood of Christ: Israel was kept together, not only through the bond of a common ancestry, but also and perhaps even more, through the unceasing repetition of solemn sacrifices with their meals of fraternity: "Behold Israel according to the flesh. Are not they that eat of the sacrifices partakers of the altar?"

Now Saint Paul is careful to avoid any word that might in the least accentuate the inescapable psychological difficulty created by custom. He is not going to encourage any sentiment but utter contempt for the old ingrained fear of the idol. The idol is simply nothing: "What then? Do I say that what is offered in sacrifice to idols is anything? Or that the idol is anything?" So there is no kind of inherent contamination in the meal that comes from the temple. But the unreal figment of Greek imagination that created the gods out of nothing is not the last word in this matter. There is unfortunately a very real evil, not suspected by the pagan, but seen by the wary eye of the Christian. Satan, evil personified, is in very truth the object of pagan worship. Devils are in the idols: "But the things which the heathens sacrifice, they sacrifice to devils and not to God." So Saint Paul by degrees arrives at that greatest of all contrasts, the cup of the Lord and the cup of the devil, the altar of the Lord and the altar of the devil. The Eucharist makes all the difference between heaven and hell: "And I would not that you should be made partakers with devils. You cannot drink the chalice of the Lord and the chalice of devils: you cannot be partakers of the table of the Lord and of the table of devils." It has been objected that the contrast loses its sharpness of outline for a Catholic because he believes in the reality of Christ's Body and Christ's Blood, while there can be no question of the blood of devils or the flesh of devils, as those evil beings are disincarnate spirits; but the antithesis, in Saint Paul's mind, is complete and fulfills its function admirably. Those who drink of the Cup of Christ and partake of the Flesh from the altar of Christ are men raised to such power and excellency that they are the true boon companions of the Lord, having eaten with Him and having drunk with Him. On the part of such as these any other companionship would be a betrayal: "Do we provoke the Lord to jealousy? Are we stronger than He?" Though there be not in the heathen sacrifice blood that is preternatural nor meat that is not of this world, there is in it a direct consorting with Satan, and such consorting is the very opposite, psychologically, of the behavior of the man who is initiated into the Eucharist of the Lord.

We must, of course, carry this matter further back and see in Christ Himself a profound and special characterization that makes Him the God of the Eucharist. Christ is essentially and personally Eucharistic, in the sense that if any mind were able to understand that most mysterious of all personalities—the Incarnate God—there would be found in Him such features of life and power and reality as would make Him most perfectly fitted to be the Eucharist in its double aspect of sacrifice and food.

The Incarnation, the Conception in a Virgin's womb, the kind of body and soul He has, the sort of life He led on earth, the manner of His death and resurrection; these all prepare Him to be the ideal Eucharist of the Christian people.

"Labor not for the meat which perisheth, but for that which endureth unto life everlasting, which the Son of Man will give you. For Him hath God, the Father, sealed."[112] This mysterious declaration with which the Son of God prefaces His announcement of the Eucharistic bread and wine seems to point to a deep differentiation of Christ's whole Person for the very purpose of the Eucharist: "For Him hath God, the Father, sealed." We all know of the danger that besets Christian thought when Christ's character is presented exclusively, or anyhow preponderantly, as an ethical greatness, as a spiritual power, though this be done on an infinite scale. Christ must be approached as One whose being is more than ethical and spiritual; He is resurrection and life; in Him there dwells the fullness of Godhead corporeally. But even in this fuller presentment of the Son of God there will be a narrowing, a restriction and a limitation, unless we see in Him also the Bread of Life that comes down from heaven, One whose Flesh is meat indeed and whose Blood is drink indeed. We may say that the only authentic Christian Incarnation is directly Eucharistic. The God who came down from heaven is also the Bread that came down from heaven: "This is the bread which cometh down from heaven: that if any man eat of it, he may not die. I am the living bread which came down from heaven. If any man eat of this bread, he shall live forever: and the bread that I will give is My flesh, for the life of the world."[113] Christ's passion and death are such as to be contained in reality in the Bread that is broken and in the cup that is drunk at the Eucharistic banquet, whether the banquet precede the shedding of Blood, as happened at the Last Supper, or follow it, as in the Mass. In other words,

Christ's sacrifice on Calvary is essentially Eucharistic, being translatable into terms of the sacrifice of the Christian altar: "For as often as you shall eat this bread and drink the chalice, you shall show the death of the Lord, until He come."[114]

The Eucharist was never absent from Christ's mind. Its final institution was His most ardent desire: "And when the hour was come, He sat down: and the twelve apostles with Him. And He said to them: With desire I have desired to eat this pasch with you, before I suffer. For I say to you that from this time I will not eat it, till it be fulfilled in the kingdom of God."[115] The fulfillment of the Pasch in the Kingdom of God is the Eucharistic mystery in the Church. The Body assumed in the Virgin Mother's womb has for the contemplation of the Church an indescribable beauty and whiteness; it is the heavenly food symbolized by the manna. With such awe does she look on its sufferings as to see in them the preparing of a holy food: "For Christ our pasch is sacrificed."[116]

The Catholic's faith in the Eucharist is faith in a life. There are no limits to life if it be left to its own powers of development.

Sow a seed in the ground and leave it to its own innate forces: its growth will cover a vast territory before a century is out; the propagation of that one seed is immeasurable. It will be checked only when other growths or other lives arise that are hostile to it.

So does the Eucharistic faith cover the Catholic world. The luxuriant growth of an American prairie would be a feeble comparison. When we accept the initial mystery of the Bread that came down from heaven and that gives life to the world, only a worldwide, a ubiquitous, an omnipresent Eucharist is the logical outcome.

We find the Eucharist everywhere, we want it everywhere and at all times. We eat daily of this Food, we have the Presence in thousands and millions of churches and chapels, we move in the Eucharistic mystery as in a garden. We are no more surprised to find the Real Presence in every place than we are astonished to see flowers wherever there is soil and sunshine.

So with the solemnity of the sacred rite at the altar the *Christianus sacrificans* unites the gaiety of healthy children in springtime, when nature is all blossoms. The *Christianus Eucharisticus* moves in a world of his own, has an atmosphere of his own, has a Presence of his own. As he goes about amongst his fellow men, as he mixes with the crowds, the taste of the mystery is in his mouth, the aroma of the Presence envelops him. A nation that lives in the faith of the Eucharist is very different from a race of unbelievers; it is a nation of strong men and women nourished on the Bread of Life.

12

The Fruit-Bearing Christian

There is no fervent Christian who is not oppressed by a sense of the barrenness of his life. He knows that he has not produced all the fruits of the Spirit which he might. Now this feeling of disappointment has nothing to do with religious skepticism; the Christian is not disillusioned in his faith, in his Church, or in his God. On the contrary, it is the hallmark of all sanctity to be filled at every moment with boundless gratitude for the gifts of the Christian dispensation, because their validity and their worth become overwhelmingly clear to the soul as it progresses. The Christian is never a *vir scepticus*, but he is ever a *vir Eucharisticus*, a man of the Eucharist. Eucharist means a mystery of thanksgiving. The Christian's disappointments and disillusionments are painful and great; they are all the harder to bear precisely because no whisper of doubt enters his mind as to the veracity and solidity of the Creed. We suffer in spirit because a tree of such dimensions, of such life and vigor, of such resistance, does not, at least apparently, bear fruit in abundance. We are disappointed in ourselves because we are so sure of our faith in Christ, of our vocation in Him, and, to a large extent, of our graces in Him; but we are not sure of our fruitfulness in Christ, in fact the poverty of results seems pitifully evident in any truthful examination of our own lives. There is indeed a most flagrant contradiction between the riches of the Christian dispensation and barrenness of spirit.

Christ has described His election of us in terms of fruitfulness: "You have not chosen Me: but I have chosen you; and have appointed you, that you should go and should bring forth fruit; and your fruit should remain."[117]

Do we not all of us feel instinctively that having received so much we also must give much? This sentiment seems practically universal, especially among Western peoples. Even Lutheran antinomianism could not be quoted as a contrary instance. Luther did not banish spiritual fruitfulness from Christian life, though the kind of psychology that underlies his whole system of justification makes it difficult to save the meaning of Christ's metaphor of the vine and the branches. That the German Reformer was disillusioned with his own spiritual life as a Catholic priest and monk seems to be a well-established historical fact; but the conclusions he drew from his personal experience were quite unwarranted. Seeing no fruit, he denied the existence of the tree; i.e. the power of the Christian soul to bear fruit in itself. For him, fruitfulness was more like the clinging of a parasite to the main trunk, enfeebling our metaphor of Christ's fruitfulness in every Christian.

Genuine Catholic sentiment is far from being so pessimistic. We all admit the spiritual fruitfulness of our brethren in Christ; to do so readily, cheerfully and joyously is a notably Christian characteristic. This lies at the root of our interest in the saints of

God; the Church expects to find in them the "hundredfold" of the harvest of grace; she does not hesitate to enter into a searching examination of the harvest of good works garnered by such of her children as may be worthy to be raised to her altars. She looks at every one of those good deeds to test its quality, its maturity, its perfection. It is indeed a bold step on the part of the Church thus to scrutinize a poor human life, the mortal life of a Christian whose existence was passed in the midst of ordinary human surroundings, expecting to find in it no single worm-eaten fruit, hoping to discover not only good healthy quality, but an almost unlimited quantity, for "much fruit" is the Church's standard of sanctity. Now we know how this keen criticism of those humble lives reveals a fruitfulness marvelous beyond all dreams; but not only the heroes, even the rank and file have full and productive spiritual lives. The barns of the Lord will have to be of almost infinite dimensions to receive all the wheat that will be garnered one day.

A difficulty seems to arise in the human conscience about our own fertility in the field of grace. We are conscious of the greatness of our calling on the one hand, and of the apparent smallness of our lives on the other. But spiritual fruitfulness is really part of our Christian vocation, and to a very large extent it is more *in* us than *of* us. We are fruitful, as the branch of the vine is fruitful— so long as it is united with the main trunk. "I am the vine: you the branches. He that abideth in Me, and I in him, the same beareth much fruit: for without Me you can do nothing."[118] The essential cause is the bond between branch and vine, between Christ and man.

The real problem is not the fruitfulness produced by that union, but concerns the nature of that union itself. What is that union? What is this mysterious quality which is presupposed by that other quality, fertility in Christ? In general terms we say that to be in a state of sanctifying grace is the very condition we want. A man in that happy state abides in Christ, and therefore has all the privileges of that union. Every Catholic child knows that sanctifying grace is forfeited by deliberate mortal sin. As such an act must be done with full knowledge and consent, a man must know when he has committed a mortal sin. This simple issue is sufficient for the purpose of realizing the practical truth of Our Lord's utterance: "He that abideth in Me, and I in him, the same beareth much fruit." Sanctifying grace is, of course, an infinite mystery in itself, still with that particular assurance that marks Catholicism we speak of its possession and of its loss with the directness of people who are dealing with personal property. We ought then to take it as an absolute axiom that none of us who is in the state of grace fails to be a *Christianus frugifer*, a fruit-bearing Christian.

No one who has the true sense of Catholic orthodoxy could find fault with the insistence on effort on the part of the individual Christian, an insistence that preachers have never failed to express. But great would be the loss to the Christian cause if the theology of effort were not subsidiary to the more important theology of fruitfulness, or if effort were considered as something opposed to fruitfulness. All our spiritual enrichment through good works is the fruit of the Spirit in us, whether those works be sweet, or bitter and strenuous. The sap of the divine life of Christ is unceasingly active in the Christian soul, and everyone in the state of grace is thereby unavoidably a *Christianus frugifer*. The multitude of such souls is like an immense garden, where everything combines to bring to maturity whatever germinating life there is. To be *frugifer*, fruitful, is as much a characteristic of the Christian as his activity. We must profess a deep and vivid faith in the universality and efficacy of grace within the Catholic Church if we would do justice to all that Christ said about His relations with His own: "I in them, and Thou in Me: that they may be made perfect in one: and that the world may know that Thou hast sent Me and hast loved them, as Thou hast also loved Me."[119]

Words like these transport us to an entirely new sphere of morality, if one may use that word here to express the phenomenon of good works (divine fruitfulness is a nearer description), nor need we be surprised at any kind of manifestation of life inside the Christian fruitfulness. The astonishing thing is that we are so ready to use the word "extraordinary" in the spiritual order, when after all the highest life is only a normal result of that radical mystery of union with God, of being in Him, of being consummated into one supreme Life. Hesitation about the power, the omnipresence, the unremitting activities of grace, is one of the greatest shortcomings of our days; yet we have the most authentic declaration of the riches of grace by the Council of Trent, the great classical presentment of Catholicism in the age of humanism. According to the Council, the faithful who are in a state of grace live in a happy abundance of good works and merits because "it is Christ Himself who pours forth His power unceasingly, into those who are in grace, as a head into the members, as a vine into the branches; which power precedes, accompanies and follows all their good works."[120]

We ought to pray for the gift of understanding, so that, as far as mortal man is capable, we may visualize this unceasing pouring forth of power into the souls of Christians by Christ. Oh, for the poet who could sing this, or the artist who could paint its true glory!

It is indeed a blessed victory of reality over mere appearances that in Christian spirituality such phenomena are considered to be the choicest fruits of sanctity as are, in a way, entirely detached from external results. The operation of the spirit itself, the thought, the act of will, that remains in its entirety inside man, may be a deed of consummate strength, and therefore a fruit of heavenly excellency. The immanent act of contemplative prayer is fruitfulness at its highest. This is why in Catholic theology we distinguish between Christian action and Christian fruitfulness, between the *Christianus operans* and *Christianus frugifer.*

In scholastic philosophy all the activities of man are distinguished into two classes: there are the *actus immanentes*, acts that stay within, and the *actus transeuntes*, acts that go out from the person. If through charity I give a cup of water to a fellow being, my act goes out of me, but in order to be highly meritorious in Christ an act need not thus go out, need not show itself in the streets and public places, so to speak. There are exercises of the spirit which excel in strength anything man puts forth outside himself, and which make him fruitful in a superabundant measure. By this we mean, of course, the whole range of Christian contemplation, from the simplest prayer of intercession uttered in the heart, to the mystical nuptials of a chosen soul with the Son of God. It is common knowledge that Christian fruitfulness is to be found chiefly in this field of the spirit; the Christian is fertile in love, this is his very life, as charity is the perfect bond that unites him with God and His world. So it will always be difficult truly to assess the greatness of Christian fruitfulness; external works, numerous and great as they are, are merely the fruits that grow on the encircling wall of the garden of God. The greater the love, the fewer the words; indeed the greatest love is inarticulate. Nor is there here on earth an opportunity for all that is in the heart of the saint to show itself in external behavior. Even if he gave his whole life to Christ, he would still feel that he had done less than the measure that is within him; for that measure is the life of Christ, not his own puny human life. The one invitation the Church may address to Christ without fear of presumption is surely that of the Bride to the Bridegroom in the Song of Solomon, "Let my beloved come into his garden, and eat the fruit."[121]

13

The Christian in Repentance

Much of our spiritual inferiority is due to our habit of being satisfied with general religious notions and terms without taking the trouble to find out exactly what they stand for in Christian thought. Words like "prayer," "sacrifice," "hope," "love," "charity," are used with a variety of meanings by all men who in any way treat of man's religion. They are the common language of mankind's natural religiosity. Our misfortune as Christians has been to attach to those terms too vague a meaning and to admit in practice that Christianity is a religion of prayer, of sacrifice, of love, in the sense in which other religions possess such characteristics, though of course Christian prayer, Christian sacrifice and Christian love are supposed *a priori* to be purer and more real. But this is not enough. We Christians are not only more religious; we are religious in a quite different sense, in a way to which the world at large is an entire stranger. The Christian prayer, the Christian sacrifice, the Christian hope, the Christian love are not found outside Christianity even to a small degree, even in a diminished form. In Christianity such activities flow directly from the mystery of man's incorporation into Christ. They are what they are through the cardinal fact that we are in Christ, and we ought to define them as the activities of Christ in His members. Thus instead of searching out elaborate metaphysical explanations of the reasonableness and the validity of prayer, we ought to be satisfied with this impressive fact: that the Son of God has prayed, has told us to pray, and has taught us how to pray in His name.

In this sense I have described in former chapters the *Christianus orans* and the *Christianus sacrificans*, the Christian at prayer and the Christian at sacrifice. It is a logical development of this theme to treat also of the *Christianus poenitens*, the Christian in repentance. In this matter, even more than in the various aspects of religion already enumerated, there is the danger of making a universal human sentiment, the sorrow for evil done, do duty for that very special grace, the Christian penitence. Now Christian penitence, duly considered, is something as original, something as fresh and as independent of man's general religiosity, as is Christian prayer, Christian sacrifice or Christian charity. The *Christianus poenitens* is behaving in a way which cannot be defined in terms of ordinary sorrow for sin. Christian penitence does not exist outside Christianity, any more than the Eucharistic sacrifice exists outside Christianity.

When we speak here of the *Christianus poenitens* we adhere strictly to the letter, we mean the baptized person entering upon the act or the state of penitence. It is clear, of course, that there is another repentance, also of a supernatural order, which precedes incorporation into Christ, and prepares man for it. When Peter had touched the hearts of his vast audience on the day of Pentecost, people came to him and to the Apostles with this question: "What shall we do, men and brethren?" The answer of Saint Peter was as clear as it was unpremeditated: "Do penance: and be baptized every one of you in the name of Jesus Christ, for the remission of your sins, and you shall receive the gift of the Holy Spirit."[122] This repentance, the model of all those sorrowings which lead man to his first justification, into the *justificatio impii*, is not strictly the Christian penitence, though it be the work of divine grace. It is only after his baptism, after his incorporation into Christ, that man can be the *Christianus poenitens*. The sins of the baptized are not dealt with by God in the same manner in which He deals with sin in general. Through baptism in Christ we are given a penitence, as we are enriched with a sacrifice; we receive a true sacrament and a heavenly mystery of spiritual cleansing. What Catholic theology knows concerning the remission of sin must be understood primarily of the baptized.

In these days of broad human sympathies one has to answer queries hardly ever formulated by our fathers. Scarcely can mention be made of God's ways of dealing with the sin of the baptized without someone asking sharply: "What about the sins of the innumerable human beings who never will be baptized?" The answer ought to be quite frank. We should say without blushing that we know nothing of God's ways with that vast portion of His human family. We only know in a general way that He has care of all flesh and that He hates none of those whom He has created. That there are truly penitent men and women in those multitudes is, of course, taken for granted. But the repentance of the man who is led to baptism, and above all, the repentance of the baptized Christian, are matters of a divine ordinance whose working has been revealed to us, and whose certainties form some of the most brilliant jewels in the crown of Christ's bride the Church. Thus we know that at baptism a man's sins are washed away forever. The pardon he then receives is without limits, without reservations. After baptism man is fit for immediate entrance into heaven, even if until then his career had been one of uninterrupted sinfulness. Baptism is the most potent destroyer of sin, but, as we have said, not of the sins of Christians.

The *Christianus poenitens* is essentially one who has to bewail his lack of fidelity to Christ to whom he has already sworn fealty in baptism. The sins of Christians are offenses against a state, the state of the redeemed. By committing sin we walk unworthily of our calling, we prove ourselves to be bad children, people who are unmindful of their election. We sin against Christ, we hurt Him in His brethren. Whether we be conscious or not of those implications, we cannot avoid having that kind of guilt on our souls every time we transgress. In his repentance the Christian has to think of many things which are exclusive to him. He has to remember his baptismal robe, he has to bear in mind his adoption as a child of God, the seal of the Spirit, the sweetness of the Bread of Life, the Blood of the Lamb, all of which mysteries he has more or less trampled under foot every time he has sinned grievously. He has saddened his brethren, he has brought shame on the Church, he has made the infidel blaspheme the Name of the Lord, he has made the work of the Holy Spirit more difficult, he has been a dead weight on fervent men and women to whom nothing is dearer than the glory of Christ.

All these results and many more are infallibly associated with our sins. Therefore when we repent hosts of invisible powers are set in motion, all demanding to be satisfied and to be vindicated. Now it is the special merit of the *Christianus poenitens* that he is determined to make full amends for all past outrages, to give satisfaction to the whole hierarchy of the supernatural order, and to repair the gap he has made in the life of Christ's mystical Body. His repentance is more than a sorrow, it is a hunger and thirst after justice, it is an effort to fill up those things that are wanting to the Body of Christ through his guilty acts. For this reason Christian penitence has become the most virile of all our activities in Christ. It would, however, be against the very essence of Christianity to take a one-sided view of this effort of the *Christianus poenitens;* he can do nothing of himself, and though it be in his power to diminish the life of Christ in himself and in the Church, yet it is not within him to make good that loss. So Christ has prepared for him the sacrament of repentance, as He has prepared for him all the other sacraments for the fullness of life.

The theology of the sacrament of penance would be an incomprehensible tangle of conflicting elements but for this fundamental assumption, that through the sacrament Christ enables His own members to make good the harm done by their sins to the whole supernatural order. So this sacrament is not defined primarily in terms of sorrow, but in terms of powers and deeds. Its efficacy rests on the one hand on the power of the keys, and on the other on the acts of the Christian, of which one only is sorrow or contrition, the others being of the executive order—confession and satisfaction. Though the injuries done by sin to the divine order of Christ's mystical life in the Church be very grievous, the sacrament of penitence is more powerful than sin. The Christian is a penitent in the true sense only when he enters into that sin-destroying dispensation which Christ has left to His Church for the exclusive benefit of His people. Sorrow external to that dispensation would not meet the needs of the case; it would not, by itself, make of anyone a genuine *Christianus poenitens.* A whole range of divine realities has been disturbed by the sin of the Christian; he cannot make matters right except through the preordained extra mercies of the sacramental readjustment. The power of propitiation that is in Christ becomes palpably operative in the Catholic sacrament of penance; and the faithful, who are the very people whose sins are in need of forgiveness, are called upon to enter effectively into that power of Christ by doing the works of the sacramental repentance. It is in this fuller sense that a Christian is a penitent. Saint Paul speaks of Christ as of one who, "upholding all things by the word of His power, making purgation of sins, sitteth on the right hand of the majesty on high."[123] This activity of the Son of God, the purgation of sins, is more than a pouring forth of the spirit of repentance into the hearts of the faithful; it is the washing away of the guilt as well as of the stain of sin; it is an atonement offered to the majesty of the Father; it is a quickening of the life of the Church which by that sin had been retarded.

More than anything else, that sacramental element which is called satisfaction is an indication of the covenanted nature of Christian penitence. When we submit to the power of the keys we are made to perform acts which have a value entirely beyond their human and external import. The Council of Trent defined that satisfaction is one of the three parts that constitute the "matter" of this sacrament of penance. Through this ordinance, spiritual deeds of a transient nature and easy to perform acquire an immense value, precisely because they are willed by Christ as a participation in His own infinite satisfaction for sin.

It is not to be wondered at that heresy has pounced on this doctrine of sacramental satisfaction as a bird of prey would fall upon a dove. Heresy is a separation, a breaking up, it is an evil genius of disintegration. It could admit personal sorrow for sin, it would not cavil at the brave act of a man who humbles himself in making the avowal of faults. But a doctrine that presupposes the most intimate association of the faithful with Christ, and the most far-reaching union amongst His members, is the very opposite of heresy. Now the penitential satisfaction of the Catholic Church takes for granted such an indissoluble link of responsibilities, be it in the sacrament, or be it in the Indulgences, which are an extension of the penitential satisfaction.

There is nothing more evident in history than the fact that the Catholic Church has invariably dealt with the sins of her children in an authoritative and public way. Her activities in this matter have gone far beyond mere exhortations to the Christian people to be sorry for their sins. She has dealt with sin as one having power and authority over it; she has remitted and retained it, in strict accordance with the commission entrusted to her by her divine Founder. She has imposed works of satisfaction according to her own discretion, she has enlarged or diminished them according to the changing circumstances of the times, she has commuted them freely from one class of works to another, she has shifted the burden from the shoulders of her weaker children to those of her stronger members, knowing that they are all one Body.

From whatever angle we visualize the Church's conduct in this matter of dealing with sin—not the sin of the world but the sin of the elect—one thing is impressed upon us most strongly; we are witnessing not so much a psychological phenomenon as a manifestation of power: the power to redress the balance of sanctity inside God's kingdom. The psychological element of heart-sorrow certainly belongs to this great healing of the wounds of the Church, but it is only one element amongst many others equally important and no less divine in origin and character. There is nothing more varied than the Church's discipline. But through all the varieties of ecclesiastical policy in applying the divinely instituted sacrament of reconciliation, two factors remain unchanged: the Church's use of the power of the keys, and the Church's right to impose penitential works of satisfaction at her own discretion. The *Christianus poenitens* has remained the same type through all the ages; he has understood with undiminished clearness that, not through his own efforts, but through the operation of a divine dispensation, through the workings of a sacramental system in which he is only a partner, justice is re-established and the balance of sanctity redressed. There are the sweet tears of personal repentance, there is the most piercing of all soul-pains, that of having offended One who is all the more lovable for having allowed Himself to be insulted by us, there is the anger with our flesh for having rebelled against eternal Beauty. These graces, for graces they are indeed, may appear at first sight to be only the intercourse of the individual soul with God. But this would be an imperfect understanding of the movements of grace. It is the Spirit that animates the whole mystical Body of Christ who brings forth those unspeakable groanings of the repentant soul. A loss is made good, and the reparation has its repercussion in heaven, where the angels rejoice over one sinner doing penance more than over the ninety and nine just men who need no repentance.

It is the peculiar spirit of Christian repentance to live by the conviction that things can be made right again in the most complete manner, however great the havoc that may have been wrought. There might be true sorrow without any such persuasion. Man could be profoundly contrite, but also deeply convinced that the wrong done will be eternally an incurable wound in the spiritual world. Now such is not the grace of Christian penitence. This, on the contrary, is a sorrow full of faith in a power that builds up everything that has been pulled down. For this reason the angels in heaven rejoice over the one sinner who does penance. Doing penance is intrinsically a rebuilding of the damaged walls of the spiritual Jerusalem. The *Christianus poenitens* is a most hopeful person as a result of such conviction. He is not like the Jews who sat by the river in the land of their captivity, feeling so desolate and shedding inconsolable tears at the thought of the distant homeland; he is like the Jews after their return from captivity, busily engaged in the work of reconstructing the walls of the Holy City which their enemies had razed to the ground. But man, left to himself, is unequal to so great an enterprise. For this reason Christian penance is to be considered as a portion of that adorable mystery of Christ, in whom God re-establishes all things that are in heaven and on earth.

14

The Christian Meets Death

Nothing is more striking than the practical working out of the differences between supernatural religion and mere natural religiousness in the face of death. It would seem that it is the special power of a faith that is truly supernatural to know what to do when death comes; and in the measure in which the pure spirit of Christianity departs, man becomes more and more helpless, gradually, in a kind of moral lethargy, he lets death creep over him. Catholicism is certainly the religion in which to die. It has a wonderful promptness of intuition in that critical moment; it knows what to say to man and what to leave unsaid; it is earnest without being fanatical, solemn without being gloomy; it has a psychological touch all its own with the dying person.

This is a charisma of Catholicism which is terribly missed by the non-Catholic, to whom the approach of death is still a dreadful thought, and who feels instinctively that there ought to be at his side a ministration specially devised for so anxious a

105

moment. The Catholic Church has always preached the solemnity of death, abhorring any levity in that grave presence. The
hour of death, in Catholic tradition, is precious beyond all words,
and the Church would see her children compose themselves into
a state of prayer and recollectedness, of contrition and hope,
which differs radically from the apathy of so many non-Catholics
at their last hour, and above all, from the nauseous levities of the
pagan world. The Church has been accused of making the hour
of death into a matter of inhuman anxiety; she seeks to stir the
conscience of the dying Christian, it is said, in a way that cruelly
strains reality and is at variance with man's sense of tolerance. Yet
this earnestness of the Church is merely the outcome of that
fundamental faith she holds that death puts an end to man's
powers of conversion. She believes that great and particular graces
are in store for the Christian at that awful hour. It is on this
account that all the ministrations and legislations which concern
the dying Christian admit of no dispensation or exception; in
practice, the one who is at the point of death has every sort of
privilege, and under no consideration can his case be neglected or
postponed. On the other hand, the dying Catholic himself is
given such facilities for making his peace with God through the
sacraments, through the prayers and the blessings of the Church
that, far from meeting his end in a state of sullen apathy, he
almost invariably awaits it serenely and without fear. In the
Catholic Church the psychology of the dying is truly a marvelous
thing, and from one end of the world to the other instances of
holy deaths are daily met with, filling the house of God, the
Church of Christ, with an atmosphere of wonderful sanctity.

It is not only the certainties of the faith that account for the
peace of soul which is a common feature of the Catholic
deathbed—a clear apprehension of the truths of the unseen world
might easily create a sense of terror—but there is an evident

unction of the spirit which seems to be the inheritance of all the children of the Church, to be indeed the reward of uninterrupted loyalty to the faith. As far back as documentary evidence can go we find that the Eucharist was given to the dying. In Latin Christianity a special name has been bestowed on the Sacrament of the Altar in this last partaking of it by the Catholic; the Blessed Eucharist is then called the Viaticum—the food for the journey—and the life-giving energies of the divine Bread are emphasized most strikingly under circumstances so solemn and so poignant. Then there is the Last Anointing of the sick, which through its very institution, is the Sacrament to strengthen man in his final struggle.

It has often been suggested that special temptations from the spirit of darkness are lying in wait for the departing soul. This gloomy possibility ought not to be exaggerated; the immense majority of the faithful pass out of this life without any signs of such acute assault on the part of the enemy of the human race. Yet that special graces are needed at the last hour seems clear from the never-ceasing invocation which the Church puts in the mouth of her children in the recitation of the Hail Mary: "Holy Mary, Mother of God, pray for us sinners, now, and at the hour of our death."

It is of great importance to lay stress on this particular ethos of Catholicism in the moment of death. There is so much unconscious paganism on all sides, and the callousness with which death is met by men and women of our time is a very alarming feature in the spiritual outlook of the modern world. It is certainly true that various races and civilizations regard death very differently from the natural point of view. The Arab, for instance, passes from life in his desert into the unknown with a light-heartedness which is absolutely baffling to a society in which every effort is made and no expense is spared in order to retard death as long as

possible. Every historian has to make allowances for this difference in estimation of the value of human life as shown by men of
diverse periods. We ourselves live in an age which has an almost
excessive regard for human life, but this is quite a modern characteristic; in most of the older civilizations to be deprived of life
was never considered a matter of so much importance as it is
today. But even when we allow for those differences in standards
of opinion, the fact yet remains that Christians of all of times have
observed the hour of death as a sacred hour; they have surrounded it with all the solemnities of religion; even if they die
lightheartedly they die holily, with words of prayer on their lips.

In spite of the exaggerated estimation of human life in modern
society our neo-pagans, by a strange contradiction—though such
contradiction is often met with both in the moral and the religious sphere—are trying to force upon us methods which are
revolting to our Christian sense. The bland word "euthanasia"
stands for a very ugly reality; the useless life, the cheerless life, even
the unwanted life, is by public authority and skillful medical art
to be painlessly terminated. Catholicism has ever made a firm
stand against all such perversities and will always continue to do
so. But, it may be asked, what exactly is the fundamental principle
on which the Church bases her conduct in reprobating as crim-
inal and monstrously sinful every attempt on human life, even
were that attempt to be made with the most humanitarian
intentions of relieving or ending suffering? Why is suicide so
heinous a crime in the eyes of Christians?

The position of the Church in this matter is simple in the
extreme: it is not a question of whether a human life is happy or
not, useful or otherwise; this matter, so supremely important for
the human race, is reduced to one principle: God, and God alone,
is the Master of life and death. If God's overlordship is denied *a
priori* I cannot see what answer we could give to the apostles of

euthanasia. In this case, as elsewhere in Christian ethics, there is only one adequate answer: the supremacy of God, the ordinance of God, in other words, the Will of God. A society completely estranged from faith in God's transcending rights over mankind will fall back on the advantages of humanity with a kind of vehement recoil, and will make of the progress of the race a religion more fanatical than any deistic religion could ever be. Let this great principle of God's supremacy be denied or ignored and there can be no restraining the teacher of euthanasia, the apostle of birth control, the eugenicist, the propagator of free love or the spiritist; all such self-styled "prophets of enlightenment" will be at liberty to foretell great bliss for the future of mankind.

Christianity has never exaggerated the cult paid to the bodies of the dead. All the civilizations with which it has come in contact have abounded in rites and services rendered to the corpses of the departed; even those races like the Greeks and Romans who practiced cremation gave great honor to the ashes and preserved them with religious love. If anything, the Church had to show opposition to that excessive cult, as it involved superstitions entirely at variance with the Christian faith concerning the condition of the disembodied spirits of men. So we find the early Christian writers pouring sarcasm over the pagan customs of lavishing gifts upon their tombs and sepulchers. One of the most delightful of the smaller works of Saint Augustine is a little book entitled *On the Care to be Bestowed on the Dead*. This charming treatise is addressed to Saint Paulinus of Nola and is in the best Augustinian style, full of wise theology, of humanity, and also of the love of the marvelous—Saint Augustine always enjoyed a good ghost story! His summing up is worth quoting: "Whatever care is bestowed on the burial of a body is not a help to salvation, but a duty of humanity, because in such care we show that no man ever hated his own flesh. So we do for the flesh of our neighbor all we can, as he is gone who would otherwise have taken care of his own body. And if such things are done by men who do not believe in the resurrection of the flesh, how much more ought such offices to be fulfilled by men who believe that whatever honor is bestowed upon the dead body—dead indeed, but sure to rise again and to live for all eternity—is in reality a testimony of that faith." Here we have the Christian attitude, a blending of the finest humanity with faith in the bodily resurrection. Saint Augustine is not over fond of privileges which are entirely local; so he says that for a Christian to be buried in a holy place, say near the shrine of a martyr, is not in itself an advantage, though those who come to visit the shrine, seeing the tomb of the less heroic Christian, may be urged to pray with greater devotion for him who is buried there.

I cannot conclude this chapter without another word on cremation. This mode of destroying the bodies of the dead is very long established in the world, and it does not necessarily imply any impiety or desecration. But it is evident that at no time have Christians cremated their dead. A writer of the third century, Minutius Felix, makes it clear that even at that early date the Christian opposition to the funeral pyre was not based on any fear for the bodies of the elect. Says he: "Nor do we fear, as you suppose, any harm from the mode of sepulture, but we adhere to the older and better custom." It is beyond doubt that the reintroduction of cremation into modern society has been invariably associated with anti-Catholic and anti-Christian propaganda, and most distinctly with the worst type of continental Freemasonry. So the legislation of the Church today is as stringent as ever. Canon 1203 of the New Code prohibits cremation absolutely.[124] If a man has left it in his will that he is to be cremated he is to be denied ecclesiastical burial, and excommunication falls upon those who would carry out or enforce such sepulture. The discipline has nothing to do with any theories as to destruction or permanence of the material elements of the body. Cremation has been chosen by the enemies of the Church as a way of showing their revolt even in death: this explains the Church's severity.

15

Christian Citizenship

More heartburnings have been caused to Christians by the problems of citizenship than by any other human issue. Citizenship in the order of nature is mankind's highest development. That vast multitudes of men should be found united in one moral and juridical person through the possession of the same citizenship is indeed a phenomenon that ought to silence forever the materialistic philosopher who refuses to see in man more than a higher sort of animal. Gregariousness may be found amongst beasts, citizenship never.

In our own times citizenship has taken hold of men like a new nature superimposed on the individual life of each member of the race. It lays its grasp upon us on the day of our birth, and not only does it shadow us till we are lowered into the grave, but it claims the right of asking from us every kind of sacrifice, even the sacrifice of our lives. We are expected to think ourselves privileged if we are called upon to shed our life blood, just because we do it as the citizens of a state, in the defense or furtherance of our nation. Into this cult and glorification of citizenship enters the Christian, as a stranger would force himself into the ranks of a well-drilled regiment, proclaiming with great emphasis the fact that he is the soldier of another king who is no friend of him whose badge the company wears. For the Christian has his own citizenship, which in comparison with earthly citizenship, is like real war compared with the play of boys. Christian citizenship is truly a terrific power, an unrelenting claim, a marshaling of souls that admits of no compromise. The demands of the two citizenships, the civic and the religious, upon the same individual constitute those heart-burnings of which we spoke in the first sentence of this chapter. The solution of the problem is farther away than ever in our own days, indeed no honest solution is possible. The Christian citizenship is a force so vehement that it will never compromise, never settle down to a *modus vivendi.*[125] It claims the whole man and it insists on molding natural citizenship with the fiery hand of a heaven-born force.

What then is this autocratic thing, Christian citizenship? How is the Christian a *civis*, a citizen? In order to have a clear understanding of this higher citizenship we must have an adequate knowledge of the Kingship of Christ. Christ's Kingship and Christian citizenship are in a way convertible terms. One is as great as the other.

Now the main feature of Christ's Kingship is its actuality. Christ is a King now, with the fullest rights and in the completest exercise of sovereignty. He will not be appointed King, proclaimed or crowned, at a future date. He entered upon His regal office in the hour in which He ascended into heaven and took His seat at the right hand of the Father to rule as a militant sovereign who is always at war. Very faulty, nay very misleading, would be our Christology if we held that the Incarnate Son of God would be made King only at the end of time, when He comes in glory to judge the living and the dead. That great coming will be more like the day on which a sovereign returns to his capital in splendor and triumph after having fought endless battles in the enemy's territory. His sovereignty was terribly real all along, as it was militant sovereignty, now it has become triumphant, but the triumph is not a coronation; the crowning had taken place, one might say, in the King's youth many years before. Christ now exerts His militant Kingship, and a very terrible power it is. Christian citizenship is neither more nor less than an enlisting in the army of that divine Warrior.

From this we see at a glance how unsparing a vocation Christian citizenship must be. This is a fact we must face if we want to enter into Christian thought: Christ is never represented as the builder of the nations of the earth, but He is constantly, and with great boldness of imagery, painted as the breaker of the peoples of this world. If Christ is a builder—and a mighty builder He is—He leaves us in no kind of doubt as to the Kingdom He is intent on raising up: "Upon this rock I shall build My Church." We may say that Christ in glory has no other political interest. Wherever we turn in the literature of the New Testament we find repetitions and variants of the prophecy of King David in the psalm of the Messianic sovereignty concerning his Lord who was to be also his Son. The power of that eternal King and Priest according to the order of Melchizedek is described in uncompromising language: "The Lord said to my Lord: Sit thou at my right hand: Until I make thy enemies thy footstool.... The Lord at thy right hand hath broken kings in the day of his wrath. He shall judge among nations, he shall fill ruins: he shall crush the heads in the land of many."[126] Whether we take the Gospels or the Apocalypse the hostility between Christ and earthly sovereignties is alarmingly in the foreground. So we could not expect the

Christian citizenship, the incorporation into Christ's Kingdom, to be something inert, something merely passive: "When a strong man armed keepeth his court, those things are in peace which he possesseth. But if a stronger than he come upon him and overcome him, he will take away all his armor wherein he trusted and will distribute his spoils. He that is not with Me is against Me; and he that gathereth not with Me scattereth."[127]

We may take it as an axiom then that our Christian citizenship must clash with the merely natural citizenship whereby we are citizens of states more or less prosperous. The phases of that conflict need not be gone into here. From the martyrdom of a Saint Thomas More to the disinheritance of the daughter of a wealthy family, who is turned out because she has done the un-English thing of becoming a Catholic, there are many variations of that same crisis: "Do not think that I came to send peace upon earth: I came not to send peace, but the sword. For I came to set a man at variance against his father, and the daughter against her mother, and the daughter-in-law against her mother-in-law. And a man's enemies shall be those of his own household."[128]

One universal principle we may state here. No Christian worthy of the name can throw himself into national citizenship head over heels, as if such loyalty were an ultimate reality, a kind of divine Absolute. Earthly citizenship for him must always be secondary, relative, provisional; for the Christian is truly the citizen of a much higher kingdom.

We said that the Christian citizenship is only another aspect of the Kingship of the Son of God. When the people of Israel transferred their allegiance from King Saul to David they said: "Behold we are thy bone and thy flesh."[129] Saint Paul presses into service this ancient formula of allegiance when he describes the relationship between Christians and their Head, Christ: "Because we are members of His body, of His flesh and of His bones."[130] It is one of the ruling principles of the spirituality of the new dispensation that in all matters appertaining to our life in Christ there is no substantial difference between time and eternity, between the period that precedes the resurrection of the dead and the aeons that will follow it. So we must take it for granted that the formula of that glorious association of King and subjects is the same now as it will be during the triumphant years of eternity: we are now Christ's bone and Christ's flesh, we are that white army which follows the Word of God everywhere, and which John, the son of thunder, saw in his apocalyptic vision. We are not citizens of an inferior grade; we are not merely on sufferance in the kingdom of the Word, we need not envy the elect in heaven, their estate as such is not a more complete citizenship, but only a more blessed condition of existence. Is the soldier in the distant countries where war is waged less a citizen than his brethren at home?

To be able to grasp clearly the significance of this civil allegiance to Christ the Sovereign, to isolate it from all the other interests that absorb human attention; in a word, to feel oneself a citizen of the heavenly Jerusalem, makes all the difference between a Christianity that is merely a form of behavior and a Christianity that is a consuming fire of the soul. When Saint Paul wants to describe the Christian life he calls it a πολίτευμα. The Greek word *politeuma* stands directly and technically for citizenship, conversation, for everything that is social life in man:

> Our conversation is in heaven: from whence we look for the Savior, Our Lord Jesus Christ, who will reform the body of our lowness, made like to the body of His glory, according to the operation whereby also He is able to subdue all things unto Himself.[131]

Such high citizenship might at first sight appear as being in entire contradiction to our present condition. Our very bodies in their lowness seem to give the lie to a claim so lofty. After all, there ought to be an external glory in the claimants to a citizenship that is all splendor and triumph. But the sovereignty of Christ which, as we have said, is the dominant factor in Christian citizenship, is so supreme that this apparent weakness is of no account. According to the operation whereby He is able to subject all things to Himself, He will also do this: He will give our very bodies the glory of His own Body.

We are exhorted on all sides not to neglect our duties as good citizens; the civic virtues are part of our ethical system. More than ever we are urged to pull our full weight in the work of relieving social inequalities and evils. No Catholic is a conscientious objector when his country is at war.[132] Catholic preachers, no less than others, find words of moving fervor to inculcate self-sacrifice in the service of one's country: if their homeland were the kingdom of heaven itself they could scarcely be more eloquent!

Are we to condemn all this civic allegiance or in some way to reconcile it with our supreme citizenship in Christ? Wise men are saying today that the heresy we are threatened with is exaggerated nationalism. The peril would be one particularly apt to beset Catholics. It would amount to this: that Catholics might be tempted to consider their respective citizenships as divine things, and give to their nation a supernatural importance, transferring to a human institution the characteristics that have been bestowed exclusively on a divine work, the Church of Christ. People, naturally, would not formulate the matter so clearly, but in their sentiment and in their imagination—all heresies have their abode in sentiment and imagination—their country would really hold such a place. We have therefore to be quite emphatic in our assertion of the merely human and transitory nature of all states. Moreover, there could not be with regard to a secular state that definite purpose of building up on the part of God which He carries out with regard to His Church: "Upon this rock I will build My Church." Secular concerns, however mighty and ancient, are subservient to His spiritual kingdom in God's plans.

Is there, then, in the mind and heart of the complete Christian, room for any of those ideals of social, national, patriotic and humanitarian devotion which now, alas! take the place of the Christian citizenship to such an alarming extent? Of course there is, and we can do all those works more perfectly if our "conversation" is truly in heaven. Charity is the bond of Christian citizenship. Now it is within the scope of charity to do all that humanity or naturalism are credited with achieving, with this difference, that there will be no excess when charity takes in hand those interests of mankind. In true Christian charity we love everything that has any claim to reality and truth. But through charity we are the enemies of illusions and unrealities because they are so hurtful to man. Our heavenly citizenship is as vast as the Kingship of Christ; in the measure in which Christ is the true King of earthly polities we also are the citizens of those polities. Where He is not King we feel estranged, we are ill at ease, and the best thing such an inimical power can do for the Christian is to bestow on him the privilege of martyrdom.[133]

In the Epistle to the Hebrews Saint Paul dramatizes this frequent ostracism of the Christian faith by secular powers. He compares it with Christ's ejection from His own city, when He passed through its gates with the Cross to suffer death:

> Wherefore Jesus also, that He might sanctify the people by His own blood, suffered without the gate. Let us therefore go forth to Him without the camp, bearing His reproach. For we have not here a lasting city: but we seek one that is to come.[134]

We are bidden by the Apostle to go to Jesus "without the camp" as if we were not wanted by an excited and belligerent humanity. Christ wept over His own city, because it had rejected Him. He is truly the divine Exile as well as the divine Sufferer. Shall we not see in that exile of His the origin of our heavenly citizenship, as we see in His death the source of our life? Knowing what a bitter thing it is to be banished from His own, He has given us a citizenship of such magnificence and permanence that it will compensate a thousand-fold for every kind of rejection by this world.

16

The Union of Souls in Christ

The thing most frequently talked of in Christianity is the very thing which is most rarely defined; if, indeed, it be definable at all. Charity is constantly on our lips, and let us hope in our hearts, yet few of us, though quite clear about certain manifestations of charity, would be ready to explain what we mean by that great virtue. This lack of clearness of outline is, in itself, not to be regretted; too easy and too prompt a definition might bring the danger of reducing within measurable circumference something truly immense. Charity is in the higher order as is life in the lower order—a mysterious reality whose manifestations are everywhere, well known, easily discerned, and whose absence is still more readily detected; yet no one can say what life is, it is always greater than its manifestations. So with Charity. We readily differentiate between the charitable and the uncharitable among men and women; a charitable deed, however transient, carries with it its own aroma, an uncharitable act hurts like a blow. But Charity is always greater than all the accumulated deeds of charity; these are only the fruits of the tree. So we need not be blamed if our concept of the nature of Charity be less clearly defined; this vagueness may argue a great reverence for the thing itself and a high opinion of it in our minds. At the same time attempts to give at least a description of Charity in its own nature ought not to be forbidden to the theologian and it is surprising to see how little has been done in this matter. Charity is taken so much for granted that it has not been felt greatly necessary to express its nature in a philosophical proposition. The descriptive method, then, is encouraged by all theological precedent, and we may well adopt it here; but the description of a divine thing, however free and abundant the use of metaphor may be, is still no small tax on the thinking powers.

As a first effort at forming some notion of the incomprehensible let us use a favorite phrase of Catholic theology; a phrase which at first sight looks more like a definition than a description, as it has all the air of great profundity: "Charity is founded on the communication of the divine good."

This is one of the favorite propositions of theologians. It contains two great ideas: first, that Charity is not God Himself, but something founded on God, something that presupposes something else, as an edifice presupposes foundations; second, that the reality thus presupposed is again not God, but the communication of God, the participation, in a created way, of the divine Goodness. It is as if our theologians said that those only are capable of the deeds of charity to whom God's Being has been first communicated, a deed of charity being, as it were, the spontaneous outcome of such participated divinity; only a being truly divine can be charitable, as we would say in another sphere that only a living organism can breathe. But there is more in this phrase: Charity is taken, not as the individual act of the individual holy person, but in its most universal meaning; that whole mighty thing, Charity, is founded on another thing mightier still, the communication by God to His rational creatures of His own goodness in the supernatural life. God communicates Himself in a way which transcends creation; He communicates His own Being, which is one, and thus makes angels and men share one life in Him, and Charity is the breathing of that life. Charity is the behavior of those who are made partakers of the divine Nature; Charity is conduct in those who are admitted to the very Table of God as His own children; its whole tenor is conditioned by this initial fact that divine life has been communicated to rational creatures. Charity is not possible without this presupposition of the divine communication.

An objection may leap up in our mind while following this initial tracing of the contours of Charity. Does it not imply that in Charity the first step is all on the part of God? Is there not in this description an excess of divine prevenience? Are we merely passive in the reception of Charity? It is good that my reader should be conscious of this feature of absoluteness in God's dealings with us when He gives us Charity. It is simply true to say that it is God's liberality and nothing else that puts our soul into a state of Charity. We cannot do it; we cannot merit it; all we can do is to work through the Charity once received; our first possession of Charity is entirely God's doing. Even when we are said to prepare our souls for God, we are passive, and not active, in regard to that final consummation of the conversion of the spirit—the infusion of Charity. So we need not feel alarmed at the boldness of this doctrine. Charity is God's own communication of His life to us as truly as a child's life comes from the life of its parents. Life is the first reality, and all other activities presuppose it; our deeds of charity, in a similar way, presuppose the initial granting by God of that supremely divine quality, Charity. We may lose Charity, but we cannot acquire it as we can lose it. If we have lost it God alone can give it back to us. We can do the works of charity if once we are in Charity; but no human works, as such, are powerful enough and worthy enough to put us into a state of Charity.

This divine origin of Charity enhances the point already touched upon, that Charity is not so much a virtue of man as the gift of God to man. Charity, more than any other thing, has this effect of fusing different spirits into one; it is its very object, its very mission. No other reality can do it, or is meant to do it; all other qualities of the spirit, be they of the natural order, be they of the supernatural order, are individualistic endowments, they are the perfection of the individual soul, they are not meant to fuse two souls into one, or millions of spirits into a united purpose. Charity, on the other hand, is essentially such a power of fusion. It does what no other virtue does, it is essentially a bond of harmony, it is the Spirit of God sent forth to gather into one the sons of God who are scattered; it is the fire that melts a thousand fragments of gold into one divine image. Charity is radically unitive; no other divine gift has this power, no other divine gift transcends the individual spirit on whom it is bestowed. Other gifts make the spirits to whom they are granted very great; Charity does not directly make them greater; Charity unites that which is already great with other greatnesses. Charity unites with God, making all our gifts so many lovely notes in the divine harmony. It is only when we appreciate this power of union that we can see this heavenly thing, Charity, in its due proportion.

Catholic theology would be quite ready to grant that a spirit might be wonderfully endowed naturally, and even supernaturally, and yet be in a state of damnation because it is not in Charity, because its gifts remain solitary, are not fused into the harmony of God, are not part of a greater whole. This, in fact, is the strictly theological concept of the fall of the angels: their sin is essentially a sin against Charity, a sin against the harmony of God's will; they are princes and powers who do not bring their crowns before the Lamb and cast them at His feet in token of their perfect communion with the Throne of supreme Majesty as do the adorers who remain faithful to God: "The four and twenty ancients fell down before Him that sitteth on the throne and adored Him that liveth forever and ever, and cast their crowns before the throne, saying: Thou art worthy, O Lord our God, to receive glory and honor and power. Because Thou hast created all things: and for Thy will they were and have been created."[135] For eternal reprobation nothing more is required in strict theology than this refusal of a spirit to enter into communion with God and the family of God, this aloofness from the Throne of God, this hardness which will not be fused into the one all-pervading life of the society of the elect.

We may ask ourselves the question whether there be not a real difference of kind between a spirituality that makes of the individual its first and principle objective and a spirituality that makes of the many the immediate aim and purpose of grace. I am inclined to think that the two are really different. If God were dealing only with individuals, as individuals, His provisions for their supernatural well-being would be very different from those which He would make for a people who would be His own people. The corporate grace will always differ from the individual grace. Looking at nature we find that God never deals directly with the individual, He is concerned with the species; the preservation of the species is the sole purpose of His providence. Are there any reasons for us to assume that in grace He has altered His dealings with created things? Certainly grace, as such, is no exception to the great law of God's created world, that the species is paramount. Grace is essentially a communication and a participation of the divine Nature in a finite way. Through its very essence it transcends the individual, and it is universal in every one of its characteristics. It makes us all enter into one common life, but that common life is one of supreme excellency—the life of God Himself. Nor are the recipients of grace, I mean human beings, individualized to any great extent. With man, as with all other species in nature, the interests of the race predominate, the individual is the servant of the race. Strong as may be man's desire for independence, he is constantly being drawn back into the vortex of other lives around him. Even in the exercise of his free will he is not liberating himself from this control of his species; he is merely doing, as a free agent, the work of mankind itself; he is neither above it, nor is he outside it, even when he acts with utmost freedom. Though at first sight it would seem that, in this matter, there is a profound difference between humankind and the other kinds of being, the difference does not really exist. With mankind, as with all other species, it is the species that predominates. Mankind is indeed a higher species, endowed with freedom and thought; but freedom and thought are essentially functions common to the whole species, concerned with the same things, with matters of human life and human death, of human goodness and human wickedness; always it is human, not superhuman or preter-human. But mankind has this feature in which it is distinct from other kinds of being, that inside the same nature there may be moral wickedness or moral goodness. This does not constitute individualism, strictly so-called, because it never allows man to avoid such punishment as is deserved by a wicked human act, or to miss such reward as is merited by a good human act. So, whether we consider the quality of supernatural grace, or whether we consider the constitutive principle of the human race, far from being driven to a philosophy of individualism, we are prepared directly for the reception of a religion that must be essentially a corporate thing.

Certainly, if we speak of the matter hypothetically only, nothing stands in the way of a spirituality which is directly and primarily corporate. Who would deny to the Holy Spirit the power of vivifying many spirits with one purpose, giving them one thought, pushing them in the might of His breath towards one goal? The many are to God as one, and one is to God as many, very much as, in another line of thought, one day before God is like a thousand years and a thousand years as one day. The Spirit is not intent on the one, He is intent on the many, to make the many have one life, one act.

We may see this more clearly if we take an extreme case of individualistic spirituality, a hypothetical case, no doubt, yet one that in mitigated form is not seldom met with. It is just possible that a Christian might consider himself as the exclusive object of divine favor. Not that he would deny that many other people are favored as he is, or are even more highly favored than himself; no sane person would question this. But his psychology would be none the less individualistic and exclusive because, for all practical purposes, he considers grace an entirely personal matter. At no stage of his spiritual development does he really consider himself as a part of a greater whole, as one whose spiritual progress is intertwined with the spiritual progress of other people, as one whose supernatural fortunes are linked up with the supernatural fortunes of other people. All his prayers are in the singular, prayer in the plural does not appeal to him; he prays, of course, for other people, for his friends and for his enemies, but he does not in reality pray *with* a whole people, with the feeling throughout that the might of corporate prayer is something far more potent than his own individual fervor. His great aim in spirituality will be union with God as the natural development of all his powers and graces, but union with the minds and hearts of others is no part of his spiritual psychology. The Sacraments are to him personal helps and remedies, the visits of the Holy Spirit are comforts to his own soul, balm to his own wounds, they do not bring him nearer to other souls animated by the same Spirit. Perhaps he even makes it a principle of his life to cling to God exclusively, as if created participations of God were a hindrance to the progress of his mind. Indeed his life would be spent in spiritual isolation; he would create around him a vast solitude, where there are only two realities that matter—as he himself would describe it—God and his own soul.

If all this were taken literally it would be very tragic. We read a good deal, of course, in the spiritual literature of the Catholic Church, chiefly in modern times, which sounds very much like what I have put into the mind of my individualistic Christian; but we know that in practice Catholic life is different, it has no such exclusive tendencies. Yet it may be said, and in saying it I do not think I am excessively critical, that in the modern style of hagiography individualistic spirituality is much more congenially expressed than corporate spirituality. Seldom does one come across passages which describe the happiness of our supernatural fellowship with other Christians; our spirituality has a tendency to be self-analytical, an attitude which is fatal, of course, to joy in the love of the brotherhood.

We may speak of Christ's mission of gathering together His elect into one; and we may give to that activity of Christ a new name: the Gathering of Christ. "He that is not with Me is against Me: and he that gathereth not with Me scattereth."[136] Saint John has a pregnant expression of his own which occurs in the very heart of the tragedy of Christ's last mortal days: "And this he spoke not of himself: but being the high priest of that year, he prophesied that Jesus should die for the nation. And not only for the nation, but to gather together in one the children of God that were dispersed. From that day, therefore, they devised to put Him to death."[137]

To be united with, to be gathered together with other elect, is a sanctification and a glory added to that first transformation of the Christian soul to which we might grant the name of individual perfection. But this link with a whole nation of predestined people, this association with innumerable saints, is more than an accidental modification of the Christian grace; it is an essential part of it. We may, at least theoretically, think of a sanctification that would be complete in the individual with no radical reference to any other creature, the relationship being with God alone. Such is certainly not the condition of the Christian. His union with fellow Christians is not an afterthought, but a primary purpose. If he were to become a castaway his rejection from the society of the elect would be as grievous a reprobation as his banishment from the charity of God.

17

The Christian of All Times

Is the Christian an enduring type? Is he of a resisting nature? Can he go on for centuries unaltered, or does he change radically from age to age, so that really nothing is permanent in Christianity except the name? We love to speak of the durability of racial properties and idiosyncrasies. Is there anything like this psychological permanence in Christians of all periods, so that it may be evident that they always remain true to type? Or must we confess to a hopeless instability, which would make it impossible for one generation of Christians to understand their predecessors?

It is a comparatively modern feature to attempt to write universal histories of the Catholic Church. Recording the deeds of holy men, and even the crimes of bad men, has always been a praiseworthy task among Christians. But it is only in recent times that men have attempted to write Church history as other men have undertaken to record, say, the history of the Roman Empire. A hundred tomes would seem adequate to hold the past life of the

Catholic Church, and the matters that could not be narrated in the pages of so voluminous a collection must be very trifling indeed. Let us praise the labors of our Church historians; they certainly have great merit before both God and man. On the whole they have been less biased and more truthful than any other historians, and they have done us all a valuable service in bringing together the visible, palpable and external facts which are like so many stones collected together, not exactly to reconstruct the house of the Church as it was in the past, but to make a road that leads from the present, right through the Christian centuries, to the very origin of the Catholic faith. The labors of the historian, even the historian of secular empires, could never be anything else than a gathering of stones for the making of a road, a road through the ages that are behind us. No amount of historic information will ever be a perfect reconstruction of the past; the best we can do is to make a causeway through endless regions that have been swamped by a flood. We may see ghosts, legions of ghosts, to the right and left of that road; but nowhere can we see real live nations in their human setting, as they actually lived in the dim distance of past ages. No generation of men is truly capable of understanding and visualizing the life of its predecessors, even of those removed by only a single century. The Church historian is one such road-maker. The causeway he constructs for us does not take us through swamped regions, but through fertile and cultivated lands, full of growth and sunshine. But he must not expect us to accept his history as anything but a road, he must not ask us to believe him to have said everything about the Church of the past. In fact, he has said very little; his role is a limited one, as even the broadest road is a very narrow strip as it winds across the fertile plain which stretches beyond the horizon.

When everything has been said about all the saints whose names are written in that book of life called the Martyrology, when the deeds of all the Popes have been enumerated, when the services of all the Christian kings and emperors have been duly recorded, what have we but a narrow road through the broad lands of Christian life in the past stretching out on the right and on the left to almost infinite horizons? The Church herself is something more vast than this; she is like the fields and the rivers, the mountains and the plains, the forests and the deserts, over which the narrow strip of solid road runs like a white thread.

It would indeed be a sad lack of perspective could we not see beyond the historian's narrative. I suppose it might be possible to number the holy men and women and even children who in any way, however modest, have an historic value and are known to the chronicler for one reason or another. I feel sure that all told they would not number many millions. These people are the historian's material; glorious material, some of it; nay—let us say it in a spirit of adoration—divine material, for Christ Himself also comes within the province of history. But who does not see how the acknowledged historic personages, with their recorded deeds, shrink by comparison into a narrow channel, to alter my comparison from the causeway to a waterway. All their achievements put together are but a small fraction of the Church's history; there is a great deal more which is not recorded, except by implication, and it is that unrecorded life of the Church I would now, leaving my previous metaphor, call the main stream. It is a salutary thing for all of us to think of that main stream of divine life which has been flowing over this earth ever since the Holy Spirit came down on the first Pentecost.

We know, of course, that there is an unfathomable depth of teeming life surrounding those salient events and dominating personalities which make up the recorded history of any country; it may be called the hidden life of the nation. Most of it, no doubt, is nothing but the commonplace existence of obscure lives;

the unending process of man's birth, growth and decay. Quite different is the unwritten and unspoken history of the empire of Christ, the Church of God. There we have a never-ceasing splendor of life, a thing wonderfully strong, an unremitting effort towards higher things, an unending struggle that is truly heroic. The famous men of Christ's empire emerge more through accident than through a positive superiority of spiritual stature. Their prominence is not always the true substance of their sanctity but, as often as not, an accidental charisma of external power and spiritual usefulness. It is the boast of that empire that its hidden life is as great, even greater, than its written history; that it endures from century to century, not through mere inertia of the human mass, but through an overwhelming though silent conquest of all obstacles, through an unceasing victory over sin and death. The unwritten life of the Church of Christ is not a stagnant pool but a rapid river rushing forward towards the great ocean of eternity. It is truly astonishing how a work so gigantic as is the sanctification of the Church through the centuries can remain so completely hidden from the gaze of men. It makes one think that theologians would be justified in numbering among God's marvelous powers the art of hiding what is great. The Prophet, it is true, clearly enunciates as one of the divine attributes the hiddenness of God: "Verily thou art a hidden God, the God of Israel."[138] The omnipresent God is also the undiscoverable God. But is there not every justification for our giving to God's hiddenness a positive and active quality? God employs infinite art in hiding, not only Himself, but also His greatest works; and in nothing has the Almighty shown such incomparable genius in the art of concealment as in the life of His Kingdom on earth.

By way of a simple test, let us take any of the old centers of the Christian faith, say, a town which has been Christ's own ever since the Roman Empire surrendered to Christianity. We know very clearly and exactly what has been the religious life of such a place for more than a thousand years. We know of the power of the Sacraments, we know all about the divine Sacrifice which has never ceased to be offered there, we know for a positive fact that Christ has been adored, worshipped, loved, without any interruption, with a continuousness of life not found in any other sphere of historic remembrance. There has been an active power, an unceasing energy, an unrelenting policy of the supernatural order, which is truly like a great river that has never failed to irrigate the countryside. And what may be said of one such colony of the Christ-life is true of innumerable other centers of the Spirit of God.

We have already given the Church historians their due meed of praise; yet no one would lead us more hopelessly into error than the Church historian if he succeeded in representing himself as the complete and perfect depictor of the Church's past. His very office of chronicler of past events ought to be a warning to us not to abide with him permanently, not to look at the historical landscape exclusively through the narrow window of his watchtower; nothing would destroy more effectually a true perspective and a healthy sense of proportion. The theologian is immensely more helpful in the work of recreating the Church's past than the historiographer. The Seven Gifts of the Holy Spirit are hardly matter for the writers of annals, yet they are the biggest, most imposing fact that has filled the world since the first Pentecost: "They are the seven Spirits of God sent forth into all the earth."[139]

The historian will divide the Christian Era into dark ages and ages of enlightenment; into years of sadness and years of joy; into centuries of spiritual prosperity and centuries of decay. But are not his criteria rather superficial and irrelevant? By the very nature of his task he is bound to confine his attention to the surface of things. What he calls darkness and failure may be very different things to the Spirit whose dwelling-place is not like the dwelling-places of men. Very often the Spirit Himself destroys the external structure so as to be more truly the Lord and the Vivifier, as the Creed calls Him. As for darkness, have we not the Spirit's own version of the true state of things?

> And I said: perhaps darkness shall cover me, and night shall be my light in my pleasures. But darkness shall not be dark to Thee, and night shall be light as the day, the darkness thereof and the light thereof are alike to Thee.[140]

In order to write true Church history one ought to know the "breathings" of the Spirit, nothing else is pure Church history, for the Church is the empire of the Spirit.

Now, we have the most authentic declaration as to the policy followed at all times by the Spirit: "The Spirit breatheth where He will, and thou hearest His voice, but thou knowest not whence He cometh and whither He goest, so is everyone that is born of the Spirit."[141]

One thing we know, however, and in this one thing the historian is extremely helpful: at no time is there an interruption in the life of the Church; in fact, when we try to give dates to our slightly fantastic periods of successive darkness and brightness in the Church's fortunes, we are constantly pushing such dates backward and forward, as we never can say quite definitely when the dark night descended. Some fact, or group of facts, unexpectedly spoils our studious map-making, and, once more, we have to change the contours of the Church's historical provinces.

But what is most upsetting to any one who wants to write the history of the kingdom of God by the same canons as those by which Tacitus wrote the annals of the Roman commonwealth is this: that the Church has a strange way at every discoverable moment, not only of being complete, but of knowing herself to be complete; one might almost say she is perfectly satisfied with herself and thinks herself the mistress of souls, nay, even the queen of the world. This happens to be the particular feature of the Church in the so-called Dark Ages; at no time did she speak with a more authoritative, a less apologetic tone. Never does the Church look forward to some future liberation, as if in the actual present she were a slave to an alien and oppressive power. Human empires have known such periods, but not the empire of the Spirit. Nor does the Church ever pray for a band of heroes to come along and lead her into freedom and victory. She seems to be conscious that heroes are with her all the time, doing splendid service in her cause. The Spirit is never without His witnesses. A good historian will himself grant that dark periods, so-called, are often succeeded, almost without any transition, by years of resplendent faith. But how does this happen? Is life born out of death? The theologian, nay even the psychologist, could tell the compiler of annals that life and light must have been there all the time, otherwise they could not have blossomed forth all at once into such power and radiance.

The only sure indication of loss to the Kingdom of Christ is the loss of faith. When a race or a nation dies to the faith there has certainly been a regression of the Kingdom of the Spirit. Apostasy from the faith is too clear an issue to leave us in any doubt as to the balance sheet of the supernatural. Loss of faith is an absolute and, ordinarily speaking, an irrevocable damage; but apostasies from the faith are rare in the history of Christendom, and they are certainly very modern. One might even question whether there ever were apostasies on a large scale before the nineteenth century, when large sections of western Christendom began that downward movement of spiritual indifference which has become the corporate infidelity of the modern masses. By comparison with this nineteenth-century apostasy the earlier schisms, and even the heresies of the sixteenth century, are things almost pardonable, since they at least evinced an interest in dogmatic matters, even though the interest were undisciplined and misdirected. But if the historian assures me—and to do this is his proper province—that Christian faith was sincerely and openly held by a people in any given country, by every rule of spiritual life I am justified in assuming that the stream of grace was flowing deep and broad and rapid, through the very heart of that nation; Christian faith could not be held without that magnificent result.

It may be objected that the historian can prove with documentary evidence that many and great crimes were committed in those periods of nominal faith, but this in itself would not necessarily argue permanent loss to the kingdom of the Spirit, as the grace of repentance may have been a superabundant compensation for the transient loss occasioned by human vice and passion. A generation that is itself poor in faith, or almost devoid of faith, seems curiously interested in the sins of the ages of faith. It is no very subtle psychological process that creates such interest. The sins of the believer are an inescapable odor in the nostrils of the unbeliever; we could not expect anything else. Nor would the unbeliever chuckle less readily if he were told that great deeds of repentance followed the deeds of the flesh; with his mental caliber he would see in repentance nothing but a mean device to escape the results of one's acts, a cowardice from which he, the virile and truthful unbeliever, is quite immune; so we must leave him alone with his illusion! But to us, who know that the Son of God came to save, not the just but the sinners, the sins of the Christian ages are no criteria of the final success or failure of the Spirit who ruled those ages.

A danger to be avoided by all of us is to become narrow specialists even in spirituality; to attach preponderant importance to definite forms of piety, to measure all things by the standard of some particular grace of our own, some form of devotion that has made a great difference in our own life. We might actually render ourselves unfit to see the greatness of past Catholicism through an excessive exaggeration of our own graces. We inwardly pity the men who were not like us, who did not do things as we do them; we forget the basic principal of all spiritual life—that it is the Spirit who quickens and leads all men. Nothing would be sadder than to see Catholic things standing in the way of true Catholicism, of true universalism. It is only human nature to judge severely those who do not share our enthusiasm of the moment, but it is Catholicism—and by Catholicism I mean here a supremely fine mental quality—to see all things in their wholeness, not just from our own narrow angle.

18

Natural Man and Christianity

The various character sketches contained in this book are, of course, the proper and, to a very large extent, exclusive features of the perfect, the complete Christian, of the man who is actually a living member of the mystical Body of Christ. The difference between the *homo Christianus* and the *homo non-Christianus* is indeed immense, one might almost think unbridgeable. Still we could not expect man ever to rise to such heights of psychological perfection as are contained in the soul of the complete Christian, if in his very nature he did not possess certain qualities that are at least remote preparations and potentialities for the higher life. Before concluding this series of essays, then, let us cast a glance at the conditions of the "cousin nine times removed" of the accomplished Christian, at man in his natural, in his heathen state. What are his chances, what his possibilities, to be more than a child of wrath?

In our own days, perhaps more than at any previous period,

good men are exercised in their minds concerning the spiritual fate of their non-Christian fellow men. It is as if a long shadow were thrown across the earth by the immense height and size of the Christian dogmatic structure; it seems to stand between the sun and a vast proportion of the human race. If Catholicism be truly the temple of God here on earth, built, not by the hand of man, but by the divine Architect, do not its very strength and harmony exclude great multitudes from being living stones in it? The more perfect and the more complete the Christian revelation, is it not also the more exclusive and intolerant? No stubble and no wood can be allowed in the work of One who has at His disposal all the precious materials of creation. For many a fervent believer the fate of the unbelieving multitudes is a shadow which almost causes him to lose sight of the sun that is in the firmament. Previous ages seem to have been much less sensitive and much less concerned about those who are outside. Saint Paul himself has a phrase that would almost suggest indifference for the man who does not dwell in the house which God has built: "For what have I to do to judge them that are without? Do not you judge them that are within? For them that are without, God will judge. Put away the evil one from yourselves."[142]

In modern phraseology this difficulty is known as the problem of the salvation of those outside the Church; it is a greatly debated question among the theologians of our own days, and it is not without interest that one watches the phases of so keen a controversy. We all seem to be haunted by the nightmare of the teeming millions who, to all appearances, are far removed from the mercies of the Christian dispensation. The burden of such a thought appears to be too great even for strong minds. So the theory has been put forward within the last few years that the vast majority of human beings are incapable of moral responsibility, and that as far as their conscience is concerned most men live and die, not as grown-up persons, but as infants.

The older thinkers felt no such need to make this world into an almost universal Bedlam in order to justify the ways of God; indeed, their attitude was diametrically opposite: they thought well of man and of his powers; they thought well, I might even say, of man's sins and transgression, because they gave them the honor of being human acts for which the sinner was morally responsible. They commonly held that man could be guilty enough to deprive himself of the mercies of the Christian dispensation. They could build up quite satisfactory theories of real theological merit concerning the eternal fate of infidels, because they believed infidels to be men and women with the ordinary human sense of moral responsibility. You cannot formulate views about the possible salvation of infidels if you start with the assumption that they are not human beings at all in the true sense of the word, being without a vestige of moral sense; you do not legislate for the inmates of an asylum, all you do is to keep them under lock and key. It is indeed distressing to see how sentiment is making cowards of us all, so that we dare no longer credit man with enough responsibility to save his soul or to lose it.

The theories I have mentioned are truly odd things; they give man a strange lopsidedness, making him almost into a freak of nature. Men may be in all other ways very competent; they can carry on commerce; they can bargain and cheat; they can show all the acuteness of well-trained minds; they can hold profound deliberations round their campfires—for we are thinking of races and tribes who have not met the European missionary; they can make war and peace; they can marry and be married; nay, they can build temples, write fine poetry, carve statues; in fact, they can do everything that makes for civilization; but one thing they cannot do, according to our benign theorists, they cannot think rightly in moral matters. They are mature human beings in everything else; but when it comes to conscience, when it comes to duty, they are no longer men, but mere babes for whom there could be nothing worse in the world to come than the limbo of infants. In this life they have played the man, both at his best and at his worst; in the next they will be like imbeciles who died without being able to distinguish their right hand from their left.

> Where are the princes of the nations, and they that rule over the beasts that are upon the earth? That take their diversion with the birds of the air? That hoard up silver and gold, wherein men trust, and there is no end of their getting? Who work in silver and are solicitous, and their works are unsearchable?[143]

Giants they were here on earth, but their souls will be mere childish wraiths. This is no ill-natured rendering of those benevolent modern theories about the salvation of the infidel. They save no infidel; for their human creatures are too incomplete ethically to be even infidels. An infidel is one who denies, not one who knows no difference between yea and nay. Their theology may surely be called grotesque; in fact it is no more theology than a treatise on infant mortality is theology. You only have theology if you deal with human beings. You may, for instance, have very good theological views on the eternal fate of those who die in infancy, whether after Baptism or without that Sacrament. Infants are normal human beings in their degree. You have principles that guide you when you think of them; they belong to the Church or are outside it, through the rite of Baptism or its omission; they are part of the human race; they share the fate of the race through the very fact of their birth. But if you tell me that an Indian Rajah, who is supremely cunning in his intrigues, who loves art and beauty, is no more than a babe, ethically, and

therefore cannot endanger his soul, I am confronted by something extremely abnormal, and it is quite hopeless to try to classify
such a strange being theologically.

Such a view, of course, when everything is said, is extremely
absurd; man is not such a monster; creation has not failed to such
an extent. Far healthier, even from the point of natural psychology, is Saint Paul's opinion of the Gentiles:

> Who having not the law, do by nature those things that are of
> the law; these, having not the law, are a law to themselves.
> Who show the work of the law written in their hearts, their
> conscience bearing witness to them: and their thoughts be-
> tween themselves accusing or else defending one another.[144]

Yes, Saint Paul knew his Gentile; he knew his Greek and his
barbarian; he realized that in their degradation they were capable
of things that would bring on them the anger of God. The Apostle's terrifying description of the moral state of the pagan world,
as we read it at the beginning of the Epistle to the Romans, has
not a vestige of those modern benevolent palliations which make
pagan sinfulness into a venial and childish misdemeanor.

> Tribulation and anguish upon every soul of man that worketh
> evil: of the Jew first, and also of the Greek. But glory and
> honor and peace to everyone that worketh good: to the Jew
> first, and also to the Greek. For there is no respect of persons
> with God. For whosoever have sinned without the law shall
> perish without the law: and whosoever have sinned in the law
> shall be judged by the law.[145]

Man's moral responsibility and ethical soundness lie at the root
of the Christian message of salvation. If Paul is a debtor to the
Greek and to the barbarian, to the wise and to the unwise, he
supposes them to be capable of receiving his message. He starts
with the conviction that they are in great peril of losing their

souls. Far from him the paralyzing impression that the world at large is essentially immature. What has he to do with men to whose consciences he cannot appeal, who are too undeveloped to have consciences at all?

We may take it for granted then, that to assume in all men of adult age the power of knowing good and evil, and the power of doing good and evil, is the older tradition. How all men receive from God supernatural grace of the more special kind, is a younger truth, nay even a more limited truth. We must avoid the mistake of interpreting the more ancient truth by the later one. If we cannot understand how God gives supernatural grace to all men, everywhere and at all times, we ought not to fall back on a theory that countless men are incapable of any higher life, in order to get round the difficulty. The one certain thing is man's moral responsibility; this we must hold if man's redemption is to have any meaning at all.

How God deals with the individual soul is not so clearly known to us; but one thing we do know: that nothing can prevent God from speaking to the heart of every man that is born into this world. The voice of conscience is the voice of God: the Word of God is "the true Light which enlighteneth every man that cometh into this world."[146] If God can illumine one human heart He can illumine innumerable human hearts. Are we so simple as to imagine that vast numbers are any embarrassment to God? When once we admit the fact that God in His own way speaks to the soul of man, we admit that He speaks to all souls, because to God all souls are but as one soul.

The modern who tries to comfort me by saying that the heathen is beyond the possibility of perdition because he is beyond hearing the voice of God, or the voice of conscience, puts before me a theological problem of much more formidable proportions than the staunch believer of the past, who says that

he does not know the ways of God with men, though he is sure
that God deals fairly with all. None of us is unwise when he pro-
fesses ignorance of all the ways of God; but is it not foolish to
limit the scope of God's power by confining normal ethical life to
a few chosen races? We seem to make God's supernatural successes depend on the number of His failures in the natural order.
Let us rather admit that all men can be saved by God, and let us
believe in the infinite resourcefulness of God's mercies. This, not
the dismal theory of almost universal feeblemindedness, is the
solid Christian comfort.

The Prophet Isaiah describes the work of the Redeemer in
words of unparalleled beauty, which Matthew the Evangelist
lovingly recalls in praise of Jesus Christ:

> Behold my servant: I will uphold Him. My elect: my soul
> delighteth in Him. I have given my Spirit upon Him: He shall
> bring forth judgment to the Gentiles. He shall not cry, nor
> have respect to person: neither shall His voice be heard
> abroad. The bruised reed He shall not break, and smoking flax
> He shall not quench: He shall bring forth judgment unto
> truth.[147]

The great and powerful Redeemer is not like a devastating
river; His firm touch is infinitely considerate and patient. Wherever there is the least spark of life, there He is patiently vigilant.
Smoking flax is to Him a hopeful sign. Far be it from Him to tread
on it or quench it. Is there anything in nature which hovers so
irresolutely between being and not being as the spark that is in
smoking flax? Flax itself is the flimsiest substance; that a spark
should not burn it up immediately shows the feeble life of that
spark. Yet there is energy somewhere in the flax. As there is smoke
there must be fire somewhere in the flimsy tuft; and this feeble
life, this most timid activity, the Redeemer contemplates with

tenderest care. Millions of human souls may be nothing more than smoking flax, but they are not on that account as nothing to the Son of God. The great Seer of the past had a true vision of the spiritual world and of Christ's role in it. His Redeemer does not move in a world that is on fire; his Savior watches every feeble spark that may be fanned into flame by the Spirit.

There is of course another, and, we might say, a contradictory presentment, this time by Christ Himself: "I am come to cast fire on the earth. And what will I, but that it be kindled?"[148] This description of Himself from the lips of the Son of God is one that has rarely tempted the Christian artist. How shall we picture to ourselves the Son of God casting fire? It has been attempted in one place, the Church of Saint Ignatius in Rome; there the Christ is seen throwing about flames. Yet strange to say the impression on the beholder is not so much of balls of fire as of tufts of flax that begin to flare up. The Son of God who came to cast fire is indeed One who watches with interest the smoking flax; His fire is the flare of flax; it is not a consuming conflagration, it is not a devastating heat, it is a great fire in the flax, coming after the smoke and the silently smoldering spark. These are the fires which Our Savior wishes to see kindled, for there is infinite patience in the fires of God.

Christ's charity makes joyful flames with flax, and illumines the world with innumerable scintillations; as we illumine our houses, not with conflagrations, but with the flickering brightness of lamps or candlelight. Man, on the contrary, in his tempestuous zeal, asks for fires from heaven to consume whole cities, and to leave them but heaps of ashes:

> And it came to pass, when the days of His assumption were accomplishing, that He steadfastly set His face to go to Jerusalem. And He sent messengers before His face: and going, they

entered into a city of the Samaritans, to prepare for Him. And they received Him not, because His face was of one going to Jerusalem. And when His disciples, James and John, had seen this, they said: Lord, wilt thou that we command fire to come down from heaven and consume them? And turning, He rebuked them, saying: You know not of what spirit you are. The Son of Man came not to destroy souls, but to save. And they went into another town.[149]

Very cold must be the heart in which there is not heat enough to make it at least into smoking flax. Can we really conceive of a man so devoid of all sense of higher things that he cannot attain that which the Prophet has expressed in this lovely metaphor of divine mercy? The wildest child of nature has ideals enough, shall I say has faith enough in some unknown Greatness, to attract the attention of the Son of God, who is on the look out for the feeblest signs of fire here on earth.

He hears the prayers of the Bedouin; He listens to the yearnings of the Hindu; He watches the conscience of the Buddhist; they are smoking flax, all of them, and none of them will He quench.

It is not granted to us to see how many of them may be blazing forth into that true contrition which means supernatural justification. But one thing will ever be to me a consoling certainty: the God who cherishes the smoking flax has power to save every man in whom there is the least spark of goodwill.

Notes

1. John 15:8.
2. Acts 11:25–26.
3. John 19:26–27.
4. John 6:67–70.
5. Luke 14:26–27.
6. Luke 14:30.
7. Luke 14:32.
8. Luke 14:33.
9. Matthew 10:24–25.
10. Luke 22:19.
11. Matthew 10:40.
12. Ibid., v. 42.
13. John 14:25–26.
14. John 15:26–27.
15. John 16:12–15.
16. 1 Corinthians 3:17.
17. 2 Thessalonians 1:3–5.
18. Matthew 10:38.
19. Romans 10:6–8.
20. Matthew 12:43.
21. Ibid., v. 44.
22. Ibid., v. 45.
23. Ibid.

24. Luke 1:35.
25. 1 Corinthians 6:11.
26. Revelation 21:23.
27. 2 Corinthians 4:6.
28. 2 Corinthians 2:11.
29. Ephesians 5:8.
30. Matthew 6:23.
31. Acts 9:18.
32. Matthew 24:27–28.
33. John 14:17.
34. John 14:16.
35. John 16:7.
36. Acts 15:28.
37. Acts 7:55.
38. John 16:14.
39. Acts 10:44–48.
40. Hebrews 9:14.
41. Acts 6:3.
42. Sui generis: the only one of its kind; unique. –Ed.
43. Luke 11:1.
44. Luke 11:2.
45. John 16:24.
46. John 8:34.
47. John 16:23.
48. Romans 8:26–28.
49. Disjuncta membra: disjointed members or fragments. –Ed.
50. 1 Timothy 2:1.
51. Ephesians 3:6.
52. Ephesians 2:18–20.
53. Ephesians 1:15–16.
54. Genesis 2:24.
55. Leviticus 5:4–10.
56. Ephesians 5:2.

57. Hebrews 9:25.

58. Ibid., v. 28.

59. Ordinary of Mass.

60. Secreta: the *Secreta* or Secret prayer was said in a low voice by the celebrant at the end of the Offertory, changing for each feast or occasion. In the contemporary English-language Mass, the Secret corresponds to the Prayer over the Offerings and is sung or recited audibly. –Ed.

61. The demonstrative pronouns that "signify unmistakable presence" are set forth below in italics, in Latin and English translation. –Ed.

> *Hanc* immaculatam Hostiam
> *This* immaculate Host
>
> *Hujus* aquae et vini mysterium
> Mystery of *this* water and wine
>
> Benedic *hoc* sacrificium
> Bless *this* sacrifice
>
> *Haec* dona, *haec* munera, *haec* sancta sacrificia illibata
> *These* gifts, *these* offerings, *these* holy unspotted sacrifices
>
> *Hanc* igitur oblationem servitutis nostrae
> [Graciously accept] therefore *this* oblation of our service
>
> Jube *haec* perferri
> Command *these* [offerings] to be brought
>
> Ex *hac* altaris participatione
> By participation in *this* altar

62. Romans 10:6–8.

63. Antiphon for First Vespers of Corpus Christi.

64. Zechariah 12:10; John 19:37.

65. Luke 22:15–20.

66. Luke 2:10.

67. John 14:28.

68. Matthew 5:12.

69. Luke 10:20.

70. John 16:24.

71. Philippians 2:9–11.

72. John 13:1.
73. Philippians 2:5.
74. Acts 26:13.
75. Luke 16:8.
76. 2 Timothy 4:5.
77. John 15:16.
78. 1 Corinthians 9:16–17.
79. Ibid., v. 27.
80. 1 Thessalonians 4:10–11.
81. 1 Timothy 5:8.
82. Titus 3:8, 14.
83. Philippians 2:30.
84. 1 Corinthians 16:10.
85. Gratiae gratis datae: The *charismata*, or charismatic gifts (which include the gift of teaching) that Saint Paul writes of in 1 Corinthians 12:7-10 are "designated in theological technical language *gratiae gratis datae* (graces gratuitously given) to distinguish them from *gratiae gratum facientes*, which means sanctifying grace or any actual grace granted for the salvation of the recipient." "Gift of Miracles" in *The Catholic Encyclopedia*, vol. 10, p. 350 (N.Y.: Robert Appleton Co., 1911). –Ed.
86. 1 Corinthians 12:2–7.
87. Ibid., v. 28.
88. Ephesians 4:12.
89. Rapts: an obsolete word meaning an ecstasy or rapture. For example: "There came a Rapt upon me, so sudden that it took me, as it were, out of myself." *The Life of the Holy Mother St. Teresa*, Book I, chap. 24, p. 165 (trans. Abraham Woodhead, 1671). –Ed.
90. 1 Thessalonians 5:19–21.
91. 1 Corinthians 14:23.
92. Ibid., vv. 32–33.
93. Bureau des Constatations: in 1883 a body called the Bureau des Constatations Médicales was established by doctors investigating the miracles at Lourdes. This was the forerunner of the current Medical Bureau. –Ed.

94. John 3:8.
95. Matthew 4:1.
96. Mark 1:12.
97. Luke 4:1.
98. John 9:3.
99. 1 Corinthians 10:13.
100. Job 13:15–16.
101. 2 Corinthians 12:9.
102. Exodus 15:3.
103. Zechariah 1:15.
104. Luke 22:28.
105. Isaiah 56:10.
106. Matthew 6:7.
107. Acts 20:28–31.
108. Ephesians 4:13–14.
109. 1 Corinthians 10:15–22.
110. 1 Corinthians 8:4.
111. Infeoffed: a term from English feudal law. To be infeoffed (more commonly spelled "enfeoffed") is to be put in possession of land (a "fief") in exchange for a pledge of service to the King or other nobility. Vonier uses the term figuratively to describe the spiritual benefits communicated through reception of the Eucharist. –Ed.
112. John 6:27.
113. John 6:50–52.
114. 1 Corinthians 11:26.
115. Luke 22:14–16.
116. 1 Corinthians 5:7.
117. John 15:16.
118. John 15:5.
119. John 17:23.
120. *Concilium Tridentinum*, session 6, chapter 16.
121. Canticles 5:1.
122. Acts 2:38.
123. Hebrews 1:3.

124. Vonier cites the 1917 Code. According to the current Code of Canon Law (revised in 1983): "The Church earnestly recommends the pious custom of burial be retained; but it does not forbid cremation, unless this is chosen for reasons which are contrary to Christian teaching" (no. 1176). Cf. *Catechism of the Catholic Church*, no. 2301. In accord with Vonier's view that cremation, per se, "does not necessarily imply any impiety or desecration," Fr. Polando, a contemporary commentator, notes: "The Church has never been against cremation as such, but discouraged it because of the reasons people used to justify it.... The Church adopted the stance it did because people were using cremation to justify denying the resurrection of the body." "Cremation: Ashes to Ashes" by Lou Jacquet, in *Catholic Heritage*, March/April 1997, pp. 22-23. –Ed.

125. Modus vivendi: a temporary agreement or working arrangement between contending parties pending a final settlement. –Ed.

126. Psalm 109 (110):1, 5–6.

127. Luke 11:21–23.

128. Matthew 10:34–36.

129. 2 Kings (2 Samuel) 5:1.

130. Ephesians 5:30.

131. Philippians 3:20–21. This passage is more familiarly translated, "Our citizenship is in heaven..." –Ed.

132. The *Catechism of the Catholic Church* addresses this issue: "The citizen is obliged in conscience not to follow the directives of civil authorities when they are contrary to the demands of the moral order, to the fundamental rights of persons or the teachings of the Gospel. *Refusing obedience* to civil authorities, when their demands are contrary to those of an upright conscience, finds its justification in the distinction between serving God and serving the political community" (no. 2242) (emphasis in original). –Ed.

133. In June 2007, Pope Benedict XVI approved the decree of the Congregation for the Causes of Saints attributing martyrdom to Franz Jägerstätter, an Austrian farmer who was beheaded in 1943 after refusing to fight in Hitler's army. Jägerstätter was beatified on October 26, 2007. –Ed.

134. Hebrews 13:12–14. In modern translations, "without the camp" is more familiarly rendered "outside the camp." –Ed.

135. Revelation 4:10–11.
136. Matthew 12:30.
137. John 11:51–53.
138. Isaiah 45:15.
139. Revelation 5:6.
140. Psalm 138 (139):11–12.
141. John 3:8.
142. 1 Corinthians 5:12–13.
143. Baruch 3:16–18.
144. Romans 2:14–15.
145. Ibid., vv. 9–12.
146. John 1:9.
147. Isaiah 42:1–3; Matthew 12:18–21.
148. Luke 12:49.
149. Luke 9:51–56.

MARK JUDGE is a journalist and the author of several books, including *A Tremor of Bliss: Sex, Catholicism, and Rock 'n' Roll*; *God and Man at Georgetown Prep: How I Became Catholic Despite 20 Years of Catholic Schooling*; and *Damn Senators: My Grandfather and the Story of Washington's Only World Series Championship*. He is the Academic Director of two programs, Politics and Journalism, at Georgetown University's School of Summer and Continuing Education. He lives in Washington, D.C.

Zaccheus Press

Zaccheus Press is a small Catholic press devoted to publishing fine books for all readers seeking a deeper understanding of the Catholic faith.

To learn more about Zaccheus Press, please visit our webpage. We welcome your comments, questions, and suggestions.

www.zaccheuspress.com

And behold, there was a rich man named Zaccheus, who was the chief among the tax collectors. And he sought to see Jesus, but could not because of the crowd, for he was short of stature. So he ran ahead and climbed up into a sycamore tree to see Him, for He was going to pass that way.

—Luke 19:2-4